by Nancy Boutilier

According to Her Contours (1992)

ACCORDING TO HER CONTOURS

NANCY BOUTILIER

BLACK SPARROW PRESS
SANTA ROSA • 1992

LIBRARY OF CONGRESS CATALOGING-IN-PUBLICATION DATA

Boutilier, Nancy, 1961-
    According to her contours / Nancy Boutilier.
        p.   cm.
    ISBN 0-87685-884-1 (pbk.) : $12.50   — ISBN 0-87685-885-X : $25.00
— ISBN 0-87685-886-8 (signed ed.) : $30.00
    1. Feminism—Literary collections. 2. Lesbians—Literary collections. 3. Women—
Literary collections. I. Title.
PS3552.08364A64   1992
811'.54—dc20   92-27428
                                                                    CIP

For Craig,
who taught me to aim high,

For Dad,
who taught me to choose wisely,

For Mom,
who taught me to see beyond myself,

and for Maureen,
who continues to help me do all three.

Contents

III. RELATIONSHIPS BLOSSOM

IV. Love Flowers

V. The Goddess Smiles

ACCORDING TO HER CONTOURS

I.
Third
Person

The Lap of Wisdom

A man who finds his way
amid her deepest secrets
does not bother her.
Those who shave pines
erect homes
dip into rivers
all share in life's creation.
But the Earth itches
under men who build roads.
She shudders at their blasts
the leveling of her ridges.
She burns under their dark brew
then she rises against the long
solid scars of pavement.
They avoid her
at her heights.
Her peaks are safe
from their hot heavy pitch
but they lay claim to lower turf
where they set lines between points
narrowly ordering the way.
Charting strict passages
they tag each gap
with a name
as if to make known their need
to fill it.
But Earth has her way
as the men and machines build
according to her contours.
Roads that brush the sky
are never straight
and summit travelers see clear
in the weave
bowing at each curve

to the goddess who is quartz one day
and feathers the next.
She stirs slopes into turns
smooths shadows into time.
The men who lay
pavement cannot hear
the sirens singing in the soil,
but Gaia rises to walk with the seekers.
She touches the strides of those
who journey without paths.
She widens the world for all
who taste valleys as often as peaks
who wander in search of both thunder and silence
who wake in the lap of her wisdom
and dream of unmapped untamed reaches.

Waxing and Waning

Because the moon's breath rustles leaves,
because lunar light climbs through her bedroom window,
because the moon must go somewhere when it disappears
        each month,
because when moonbeams dim, starlight's luster carries on,
because she has trouble sleeping alone,
because to the moon she prayed when she fell off-cycle,
because men have left footprints on her too,
because she hasn't slept well since the clinic,
because each night she watches expectantly as the moon
        grows to fullness,
because emptiness follows fullness,
because each time she counts stars, the number increases,
because she never believed it was a man in the moon,
because the ones who don't reach earth must go somewhere,
because poverty is a miserable father,
because she must love herself before she can love another,
and most of all, because it hurts to recall loss without hope,
she lies awake at night wondering which nova is her child.

Ghost Stories

"They won't believe you anyway."
She tried to pretend they were playing,
but her brother had no smile, ignored her tears.
He just toyed with her fear that Dad would hit them
if they disturbed his sleep after the midnight shift.
So she let her brother lift her skirt,
touch her and lead her hands through
daytime cellar dampness.

At night sometimes
he'd crawl beside her
and she'd wake to find him
fingering inside
and whispering, "Little Pig, Little Pig, Let me in."
Then, he'd place her hand so she wanted to scream
and hardened himself in her six-year-old palm,
reminding: "They'll say you were only dreaming."

An Obscene Phone Call

911
She dials the phone
Nine-One-One
"I am so sorry," he whispers
so softly
his words sting more than his fists.
"I'm so sorry, babe,"
he sings again
so it sounds like the refrain
of a love song at the far end of the FM dial.

"911—Emergency Aid,"
a voice like an impatient librarian's,
"Please give me your name and location.
Hello? Can you tell me where you are? Hello?"

"I won't ever again, honey.
I never wanted to hurt you.
I'm sorry. I'm sorry.
Hang up the phone, babe.
Hang up the phone and come here."

Her front teeth move slightly with her tongue
as she assures the operator
and herself:
"He says he's sorry."
She answers his call.
The operator hears a click,
a dial tone.
She has heard it all before.

Objectively Speaking

Evil temptresses of the world
inviting rape,
it is no wonder that you provoke
such violence against yourselves
since your vile nature
has been made so clear to you
for so long.

Daughters of Eve,
you must know by now
that your fathers have been blameless
when they have raised themselves against
or on you.

Yo bitch,
your sinister ways
fetter their freedom.
Only when you are the source
of their powerlessness
do they release their righteous rage
in your direction.

What were you wearing
when the defendant saw you that evening?
Why were you out so late, alone?
What a pity—running in the park
when it's dark, in the city.

Wicked women,
you must claim the shame
you bring to every man
who has ever fallen prey
to your enchanting ways.
You must nurture the self-hate

20

taught by your fathers,
treasure your guilt—
a gift from your brothers.
"Your desire shall be for
your husband,
and he shall rule
over you."
Amen. Amen.
You will beg for it,
plead for it,
and love it.
Amen.

Voices Like Frying Pans

Voices like frying pans
speed heavily across the room.
Screams, shouts, curses, tears
cut conversation beyond
comprehension.
She wants only the children.

He used to talk gentle.
Words danced from his lips
and she was soft in his hands.
The first time they woke
after tongues thighs torsos flesh on flesh
even the morning taste of tobacco on his breath
lit a fire in her when they kissed.

First time they slept with baby nestled beside them,
his dreams were wet with the taste of milk
and he embraced her with the softsmoothsweetness of honey.
The first time they slept after a fight,
she let him have his way
knowing there was anger
not love
in their hold.
She lied to friends
about the swollen eye,
hoping it would pass,
but the swelling she felt inside
scared her,
and she knew
it would outlast the bruises.

The first time he slept somewhere else,
she prayed that he'd sleep there forever,
so that the swelling in her

22

could be her own.
Now he wants the house,
he wants the money,
and all she wants is the children.

The Fortunate Ones

The fortunate ones bear scars
of physical healing.
They wear high-collar blouses
to cover knife lines,
shorts over swimsuits
to conceal marks on inner thigh
where belt buckle tore skin.
They misname their maiming
for their daughters and sons.
"Here's what can happen
if you ride two on a bicycle,"
says someone's mother
(who was once someone's daughter)
as she rolls up her shirt sleeve
to an eight-inch seam on her forearm.
The fortunate ones bear scars
that look like childhood accidents.

The Dancer

She had been a dancer too long.
Laced in silken slippers,
wrapped in leotards and
legends of handsome princes
who admired supple arms and
sculpted
thinness.
Strapped in her own grace and beauty,
everyday flying, whirling, eyeing herself
in a thousand mirrored flashes of flesh and limb
across wooden floor, reflecting back
wrist, neck, thigh, spine-erect and head held high.
She was everything, everywhere,
beautiful.

Recitals and curtain calls behind,
years later, she camouflages thickened thighs
in tents of floral patterns and tie-dyes.
Battling female form, hiding Rubenesque shape,
torturing herself with store fronts,
she pretends to admire new fashions,
while mannequins mock her
with their posed perfection.
Searching for styles,
she tries on clothes
three times the size she wore
when she kept herself starved
and rib-caged
and beautiful.

She pirouettes before changeroom mirrors,
cursing the color, the cut, the fit.
Folding arms to cover breasts
she never asked for.

Wanting to smooth the cottage cheese flesh
that has stolen away the lines
of muscular length.
Not able to undress
far enough.
She buys nothing;
no one is selling
what she
wants.

False solace in an ice cream sundae,
followed by a piece of double-chocolate layer cake,
and later still, a dozen oatmeal cookies.
Returning to her bare apartment
where bathroom mirror tells her
the room is empty no longer.
Too full.
Seeing herself grow broader, bloated,
her imagination steals away sight.
She visions a thin self
leashed in a body
not her own.

Alien costume
constricting
further,
until
she explodes.
Vomiting anger.
Retching between hope and none.
Alternating silence and echoing cough,
as if to rid her of herself,
her imperfection,
her self.
Purging to the point of hollowness,
wanting to dissolve or, at least, disappear,
the dancer slowly lifts her head,
leans forward on ceramic sink

and sees her flushed face steadying
before her on the shelf.
Washing residue from lip,
she sees in the mirror
that she is
still
there.

Jonestown

She spoke like she was apologizing
for the fact that she breathed.
He moved to her
as if in a science fiction thriller,
hunched and silent,
organ music in the background.
He touched her with a softness
that warmed her kidneys.
She moved with him in ways
that can only be explained
through senseless metaphors.
They loved one another long
enough
to agree
on a dual
suicide.

Sistervoice

It was carved in stone
on walls that caged Cassandra
within the echoes of her own words.
It was drowned with the women of Salem
who suffered for the ignorance of their priests.
It is found in the ashes of funeral pyres bright
with the burning flesh of Hindu widows on the Ganges.

The truth speaks
and is not heard.

Free speech falls on granite ears.
Taxation without representation
evolves into a womanless Senate.
The world makes little room
for the words of the poor.
Our brothers do not want to hear
our stories, our myths, our truths.
But in the minds of the imprisoned
freedom finds voice.
A phoenix rises in the lives of women
and with the words of their lives.

Sisters, be witches, shamans and seers.
The prophetess in each of you
sings for us all.

If the Pentagon Had a Price Club

Shopping for melons:
So many, so fresh, red as blood.
I reach for the first and shake,
not sure what I'm supposed to hear or feel.
I take another and shake—listening, squeezing, comparing.
Big, round, smooth and soft. How can I tell if it's ripe?

For cereal:
I read labels.
Calories, bran, all natural,
Fortified with vitamins and minerals.
I still enjoy the hidden treasures inside,
like spy scopes, decoder rings, and washoff tattoos.

For cars:
My father taught me
what his father taught him,
Buy American and shop according to need.
Power under the hood, a comfortable ride,
and room enough for the entire family.

For weapons:
Speed of deployment,
Strength of detonation.
Rate of destruction.
Quality of pain.
Effect on unemployment,
Renewal of government contracts.
Minimum and maximum firing range,
Longevity of toxic rain.
What death song will it sing?
What color is their skin?
How many will the system kill?
How many will it kill?

Weekends at the White House

The President is spending
Saturday morning with his grandchildren.
The room erupts with delight
as Roadrunner escapes
and Wiley Coyote blows himself up again.

Cartoons give what
life does not allow:
battles with a single point of view,
falls that flatten without killing,
explosions with temporary ash.

When Tweety tinks he tees
a Puddy Tat, sure enough,
it's a hungry feline,
and the perceived threat
is a threat indeed.

When Elmer J. Fudd
aims his shotgun
Bugs calmly plans retaliation.
Who can blame a bunny
for fighting back during rabbit season?

Mr. Magoo's lack of vision
is rarely a problem
(unless you count
racial slurs made
at expense of Charlie the Chinaman).

Saturday morning colors
steer clear of grey
and distill all conflicts into

black and white,
filling the childmind with easy choices:

Good guy turtles and caped crusaders
embody daring, righteousness, invincibility.
Enemies identified
concretely
by scars, accents and evil sneers.

The President is spending.
The room erupts;
a threat indeed.
Lack of vision, evil sneers
and the childmind has easy choices.

Behind the Billboards

Picasso looked inward to find the color, shape and spirit of human form. Millions view his brush strokes in the hope that they will see what Pablo saw, as if to decode genius in art is to know man and mind behind it. I turn my eyes outward to find shapes that nameless, ordinary people want to see themselves take. Then I sell it all back to them in small, square packs: menthol, filtered, and light. How can anyone resist a giant stylized cock-faced camel that plays Vegas, drives a Harley, shoots pool, windsurfs, looks like Bond, and always smiles while offering up the longest in his pack? Unadulterated masculinity for modern man rolled in the smooth character of his smoke and available by the carton. Find me a guy in a cigarette ad with nothing between his legs and I'll show you a butt that doesn't sell. For ladies, it's the latest fad in diets: Superslims are in to say you've come more often than a long way, baby. The only way is all the way, as she puckers lips of red, wet, oval begging all to take a long, hard draw. I dress her up and down, free and flashy girl in mile-high style, pretending to be casual and healthy. Always spindle-thin and packaged in distortion, inviting all to take a crack at her. Stretched and twisted, she fit the frame my anorexic ex-wives saw in full-length mirror. Like Picasso, they looked inside as much as I look out for true proportions that sell. I have studied each for knowledge of desire, and now, both archaeologist of market research and craftsman of images, I build empires to feed hungers just long enough to fuel appetites for more.

The Common Cold

Killer Koolaid on ice.
Body parts in the freezer.
Ovens to fry those who have
other gods.
Some disappear
even before the death
squads wake.
Others face execution.
Surgical bombings.
What a way to cure
the common
cold.
No
new taxes.
I earned my place
in the suburbs,
in the suburbs,
in the suburbs,
body parts in the freezer.
Ice to fry those who have
other gods.
Killer Koolaid
"Helter skelter"
smeared with
blood
on walls.
On walls
where portraits hang,
decisions are made to cut off
funding.
Some disappear
even before
anyone at the shelter wakes.
Others face life

without an immune system
or information about options
for pregnancy
while the execution
of budget cuts
becomes as artful
as surgery
and as sterile.
What a way to cure
a recession,
to earn a place
in the suburbs
with
blood
on
hands.

The White Whale Speaks

Whatever gave that hollow-faced fisherman
the idea to stake such a reckless voyage
on my capture I'll never know
but I can tell you now:
he was his own worst enemy.

I have more in common with him
than with the myth he made of me.
I breathe his air
I protect my kin
I fight for my own survival.

But he made me into something I am not
never was
never will be
some idea incarnate
an abstraction made flesh.

He carried on with such obsession
even after he hung his own leg
in a noose he's strung for me.
He carried on with such obsession
to destroy all that he could not subdue.

Any force that failed to follow his will
he branded as other than himself
and having grown so big
in his own mind
he could not tolerate otherness in any form.

Whatever evil he saw in me
was cargo of his own.
But one captain's crooked fever

burned a price tag on my brow.
He carried on with such obsession

others took it to be a truth.
They joined him in his wicked blindness.
They shared his twisted load.
They took me as their target
and never felt their hearts corrode.

He carried on with such obsession.

Let him and all men like him
keep their harpoons
to themselves
or else perish
on the points they hone for others.

The Moment of Take

Only in the moment of take
does truth emerge.
Silky feathers mask
talons on the underside
of a soaring hawk.
Hungers hide themselves
until a strike.
A waiting frog holds his tongue
long enough to feel the stir
of a fly within reach.

But hunter often turns hunted:
Preparing to unfurl his devouring tendril
upon the buzz of supper,
the almost-prince
finds himself unseated
from his mud-caked kingdom
by a flash of feathers and claws.
Legs flail
tiny heart beats so rapidly
that blood cells scream
and echo off the lily pads
to no listening ear.

The Truth About High Heels

She wants to be someone's protagonist
who takes over when Jane Eyre
sells out to Rochester.
She wants to share the limelight
with nobody and live in pages
that never compare or contrast her
to some evil or wonderful
step-sister or mother
or mad woman in the closet.

She wants to build bridges over
menstrual rivers, escape the dangers
of fire-breathing dragons, and chase
the phases of the moon through galaxies
of glass slippers until she finds
the truth about high heels
and realizes that shoes
do not change in size
but feet do.

She wants to grow tall in wheat fields
celebrating rain and sunshine and frost,
dew and wind and starlight alike.
In mid-night hours, bare feet
and loose breasts will dance
through the golden stalks
half-hidden in a shield of mist
until her legs take root in the land
and her arms embrace the clouded sky.

If and when the story must end,
she wants the heroine to be enough.
The theme can be neither love,
nor relationships, nor god—

but one woman,
detached and
independent,
strong and
feminine.

So she begins to write
and discovers she has spent too much
translating the language of heroes
to fit her own life,
telling herself that "Everyman"
included every woman,
and that every hero might have just as easily
been black or female or fat,
but simply never was.

Her heroine grows to be independent,
strong and feminine,
but not detached.
She finally sees why no experience
can presume to fit everyone's life.
Only the eyes of one never excluded, by life or language,
can frame a character with Everyman's bold assumption that
        any
woman should make the effort to feel included
when she isn't.

She decides to leave Odysseus on the dusty shelf
and James Dean leaning on his lonely wall.
She does not want to be immortal and alone.
Instead, she sings songs to her sisters,
she inks graffiti on restroom stalls,
she whispers rebellion
when she finds her own voice
and believes her own forms
to be heroic.

She writes, not of conquering,
not of killing.
The cost is too great
if she must eliminate others
to exalt herself.

She tries to write only of herself,
but so many voices emerge.
She cannot prevent her heroine
from reaching out to the others.
Relationships blossom.
Love flowers.
The goddess smiles.

She wants to write in the third person,
but I can't.
My experience is simply that,
and I mislead if I insist
that we can take it to be ours.
I ask far too much of you
if I expect you
to squeeze
your story
into mine.

I have lost the novel,
the poem,
and the protagonist,
but I have found
my own voice.

The Climb

It's only the uphill ride to work that gets me thinking about writing letters—letters to my mother, to my college roommate, to my former swim coach, to Michael. By the time I ride my bike home from work, the summer sun has fried my energy for dealing with the present, so there's none left for dealing with the past. I reek of chlorine, and I can still hear my whistle screeching, my own voice echoing in the umbrella that protects me from the heat of the summer sun: Bleeeep! "No running on the deck, you'll get hurt!" Tweeeek! "Tommy, don't dunk your little brother!" Preeeet! "One more cannonball from you Caroline and you're out of the pool for the afternoon!"

Long before the sun commands the day and the kids fill the pool, I rise, stretch briefly, shoulder my bike down the porch steps, and with one foot on pedal, I push myself to a long easy glide. Then, leaning forward, I throw my other leg up and behind me, over the seat, for the perfect mount, coasting as far as I can before I begin to pedal. The morning ride to the country club gives me a full hour to begin the day where I have left off the past. I get a good four miles of flat terrain in the valley when the light is still locked behind the mountains and the cool New England chill mixes with the shadows to ease me out of morning's warm embrace of sleep. The beginning pace is slow enough that the wind woofing in my ears does not drown out the rappling of the river as it spills softly along the roadside. The mourning doves still sleep on the telephone wires at six-thirty, and robins are too busy fishing for worms to notice me. No cars at that hour either, so it's me and my regrets peddling southbound along the state highway that winds through the Berkshires.

I'm usually at the turnoff to the mountain before realizing how deep in thought I am. As I glide into the right-hand turn and head up toward the gap, I face the west with the sun edging up behind me, and it'll be another mile of easy, gentle riding before the nine-mile climb begins. The shadows grow more distinct as the black of the road shines almost white in the light contrasting with the patches of dark shadows that mark the spots where trees along the road block the sun. By now I have already addressed my first letter. Today it is "Dear Michael." What went wrong, I want to ask him, but that's far too direct, so I ask how are you, do you like New York, are you still trying to get into business school? I will not ask about Marianne. She is beautiful according to a mutual friend, and I imagine her tall and blonde with hair evenly poured over her shoulders, like the women of shampoo ads. She is everything I am not—elegant, graceful, serene. She has high cheekbones, a smooth, flat stomach and round, full breasts.

As the incline steepens and the road begins weaving its way across the mountain, it is to my mother I am writing. She looks like an older version of me—strong and stocky, thick calves, a high forehead and long, oval face. I am trying to tell her that yes, I've made love. Not just the high school fooling around to know what it feels like, but after that, in love. Mom, I wish you could have gotten to meet Michael beyond the Hello-how-do-you-do at graduation. It was enough to handle you and Dad together for the weekend. Michael puts cinnamon in his coffee and mustard on his fries, but he's a traditionalist at heart. He carried a watermelon in his backpack for two days just so we could eat it atop Mt. Washington. Mom, remember our own days hiking in Zion? You had just moved out to Phoenix after the divorce. Laying side by side on that rock ledge deep inside the canyon, we looked up at the sky and invented new constellations. I would read by flashlight from my astronomy book: "The Big Dipper," and you would look around naming what you saw: "The Coffee Dripper." I pointed to "Orion" reaching out as if my fingertip could pinpoint each of the three stars that made up his belt. "Orion's Belt" I exclaimed. Then you traced out a long line of stars and identified "Orion's Balls." We laughed, and then I asked you what it would feel like to be with a man. You told me not to be scared, that it wouldn't hurt. It could be beautiful, you said, and Mom, it was. But it hurt, too. That's what I really want to tell her, that I am hurting now.

44

I am in a low gear, my thighs are burning as I hit the steepest section, the last three miles to the peak. The sun is hot on my back and shoulders, and I look down only at the asphalt before me, trying not to swerve. My legs spin quickly, but the bicycle only inches its way forward. My stomach tightens and my hands are clenched fists on the handlebars as my weight shifts on the seat. Sometimes, I am actually off the seat stepping alternately on each pedal until it feels more like climbing stairs than riding a bike. My arms are bronze and sinewy from sunshine and swimming. I watch the muscles in my forearm harden as I pull on the handlebars against my own weight. The shadows dance lightly and unevenly on the tension in my arms. Directly below my front tire is a shapeless blob of black that outlines bike and body bobbing along the pavement.

Now it is my college roommate, Karin, and I am asking for advice. No, too late for advice, Karin, what I need is support. The way you held open your coat pocket for me to throw up in when the bathroom at Sigma Phi had a mile-long line. You stood next to me telling the foulest jokes when I had orthoscopic surgery on my knee. It hurt to laugh, but I loved you for every smile. And you held me all night after that teaching assistant cornered me at his apartment when all I wanted was some extra help on my Cuban Missile Crisis paper. Karin, you know I'm not ready to marry Michael, to marry anyone, and if I had told him, marriage would have been his solution. You were always the worldly one, the one who knew how to get fake ID cards in the combat zone and how to break into the observatory so we could look into the "Top of the Hub" restaurant and watch waiters serve wine upside down in the telescope or peer into the lighted windows around campus. One night we saw two women kissing, and we talked all night about what made friendship different from love. We both feared we could never be as close to any man as we were to each other. Who are you close to now, Karin? Did you know that Michael used to tease me by claiming the only reason he was seeing me was to get to you? The "we" of Michael and I always included you and the rest of our gang—Mimi, Linda, Steve, and Swifty. We couldn't take you all with us after graduation, and maybe Michael and I weren't enough for each other. We'd already broken up—he'd been seeing Marianne for almost a month by the time I knew what I was feeling. Oh, Karin, was I right to decide on my own? I felt so alone. I couldn't tell him. I couldn't even tell my mother. It was better to get it over with as soon as I could.

I think of Michael again. Legs and back and body burn with the mixed heat of my own movement and the sun's growing intensity. My shadow will grow longer, and I will be able to separate the bike from the body as I continue up the mountain and the sun climbs the sky. I watch with vague recognition that it is both a shadow and a reflection I see before me. Michael, I will always love you, but you were right about us, and even when I miss your habit of burrowing under my armpit and surfacing again with your big brown eyes wide and wanting, I know we have moved on for the best. We couldn't hike off all those distractions. The week before exams, we cut every class, you strapped our lacrosse sticks to our packs, for walking sticks, you said, for fighting off bears. Serious conversation carried on while playing catch across rivers. You or I finally scuttered across the wet rocks, playfully dragging each other into the water, and we dried ourselves with the warmth of making love. We gave as well as we could, but enough would have meant much more. A baby would not have made up the difference. But I never wanted to act behind your back. Someday you will have plenty of children with some other woman who will love you too.

I taste salt on my top lip as sweat mixes with tears and each pedal makes me think I cannot stand it any longer. I see my swim coach and I am eight years old again, crying as I try to cut through the water faster than last time. I touch the wall and look up to my coach who frowns at the stopwatch in his hand. He is handsome. I want to marry someone just like him. I will work harder, stop eating ice cream, ride my bike to and from practice. "Lazy kick" is all he says, and I have to swim it over again. I can stand it no longer, but I never even consider stopping, resting or walking my bike. The forest is thick near the

46

summit and so the air is cooler and darker, but I don't recognize the darkness as shadow because there is no room for sunlight to break through the trees with the offer of contrast. No room for thought now either, only motion.

As I round the final bend in the road, a bright blue wedge of sky crowns the asphalt, dividing the pines. I am wishing my mother could see me here, at the top. I am strong and persevering. I see her at the pool side smiling, clapping her hands. Her hair has not yet turned grey. Dad is somewhere on business. I bend for the race director to put the medal around my neck. My coach nods, winks and sends an approving smile my way. My skinny twelve-year-old legs are trembling from excitement, fatigue and chills, but I feel as big as a tree. Mom, I miss you. We have always known how to laugh together, but I wonder now if I know what makes you cry. The pavement disappears on the other side. What has been seen has still not been reached, and I must pedal on. I am both there and not there yet. I feel all the energy surge and in that moment the illusion of letter writing explodes and I see them all—people I have given to, who have given to me. They appear and dissolve as quickly as the need to pedal because I have crossed the peak's crest and the bicycle takes over as it spins forward, coasting and building speed. I collapse into myself, and exhaustion settles deep in my bones.

The country club is two miles down the backside of the mountain. My shadow is stretched way out in front of me, the lines of my body distinct, my shirt sleeves fluttering in the wind. Even the loose curls of hair that flap and dangle out from my helmet are visible in the shadow. I see myself intact, complete, larger than life. My inner voices fall silent as wind fills my ears. I look and listen to life rushing around me—green and bright and morning and the music of birds. I cool quickly. Sweat dries. I am marked with no signs of the uphill struggle by the time I slide in the driveway and roll, effortlessly, through the gate.

I greet the tennis pro cheerfully, wave to the woman opening the snack bar, wink at the young red-haired boy who cuts the grass. After unlocking the pool area and testing chlorine levels, I assemble the giant hose, turn on the powerful suction and vacuum the pool before the children arrive.

For the rest of the day, I will sit in my protected chair and blow my whistle, saving children from their own recklessness: Bleeeet! "No running on deck, you'll get hurt!" Tweeeep! "Tommy, don't dunk your little brother!" Preeeek! "One more cannonball from you Caroline . . ." Although I am shielded from the sun by an oversized umbrella that cloaks me in darkness, my whistle, my bright orange bathing suit and the red cross posted on the towering chair signal to everyone that I am the lifeguard on duty.

II.

To Throw
Like a Boy

To Throw Like a Boy

*He whose testicles are crushed or whose male member is cut off
shall not enter the assembly of the Lord.—Deuteronomy 23:1*

Despite appropriate estrogen levels,
I learned at an early age
to throw like a boy.

When Billy Lester cried
for being chosen last
the other boys called him a girl.

As we grew older
our language grew richer.
"You woman," hissed Brad Seeley
when David Matsumura walked away from a fight.
I was better versed in cussing
than body parts by the time I was
singing the neighborhood slang.

"You pussy," I screamed at my brother
when he refused to play me one-on-one.
Although he had 6 inches and 40 pounds on me,
he cringed at the insult, accepted my challenge,
and I stood my ground when he drove to the hoop.
I don't remember slamming asphalt,
but I came to hearing the compliment
"Man, your sister sure has balls."

Such flattery ran dry
when I hit the age of Kotex.
Without words for rhythms
my body understood
I had to choose

between exile into womanhood
or their loudest praise of me,
inclusion as one of the guys.

Unsexing myself was easy at fourteen,
but fourteen lasts only one year
and the swelling of breasts
tingling between thighs
put me at war with my body.
Too much ambition, too little food—
going to every extreme to avoid being
without balls, a pussy, a woman.

Beyond Biology

Legs splayed open
Body stiff
The smell pushes me away
But I press on
To prove I'm as tough
As the boys.

"It's a girl" I pronounce
About the formaldehyde frog
Sliced and pinned open before me.
Three razor-blade incisions
Unlock the frog from chin to crotch.
The colorful arrangement of amphibian guts
Dyed bright by chemists
Looks like a snak pak box
Of Fruit Loops and I say so.
Mrs. Germaine frowns and from across the lab
She asks "How do you know it's a girl?"
I point to the frog before me:
"The black scummy stuff—it's eggs, right?"
She nods and asks me if I'd like to tell the class
How I know.

I tell them about firecrackers:
How if you time it right
The frog explodes mid-leap
And if you're slow to get away
The guts get in your hair and on your clothes.
Especially the eggs—they go the furthest.

"You don't really put firecrackers in their mouths"
Mrs. Germaine tries to persuade me
But the giggles of classmates call forth
My stories of the frogs we hung

In a pine tree down by the swamp.
"Like statues" I say
And then I tell how easy it is
To pose dead frogs
After you knock them on the head
Before rigor mortis sets.
"You can freeze 'em for good."
I go through the whole collection:
The Lovers sitting at the base of the tree
With their webbed arms entwined,
Wild Bill Frog suspended from his tiny noose
And an acorn cap folded into the frog palm
Of The Discus Thrower "classical style," I add.

When I get to Jesus Frog
Nailed to a branch near the top of the tree
The look on Mrs. Germaine's face scares me.
I see no anger, but I figure I'd better turn
Attention back to Biology class and the frogs
On the table before us:
"Hey, a dead frog's a dead frog.
No difference if it dies with chemicals,
Firecrackers or just knock on the head for posing."

Mrs. Germaine's face is frozen
It's not her usual "Go-to-the-principal's-office" face.
It's sheer horror,
And I've never seen horror
So fully invade a face before.

That's when I see them—
Little green spirits
Webbed and bubble-eyed
Rising from the lab tables.
No one else can see them
Or hear the hoarse croaks
That call forth the frogs we hung.

Remembering Nana

      I remember the pattern engraved in her spoons, the arms like lion paws on her chairs, the way her sugar cookies melted on my tongue. I have held onto her stories of the board-walk in Llandudno, the penny arcade, the rocky Welsh shores of Caernarvonshire. I carry melodies she brought across the Atlantic when she was eight. Songs sung with gruff syllables and words meant to be coughed. I remember the high notes she blasted beside me on Sundays when we shared one hymnal and a thousand prayers. I remember straining on the tips of my toes never reaching the high notes she hit with ease.

      I remember the sweet hot air in the attic where I shuffled through hat boxes, racks lined with wool knickers, plaid shirts and brittle crinolines. I would lean up and into the pipe that carried my voice to the sitting room and hollered to her my list of collectibles as I discovered each gem. A ceramic pirate you could drink from, a plaster of paris poodle she said my father made when he was my age, a gold locket that opened to a tiny black-and-white photo and a flash of reddish hair. I bounded downstairs to have her lace me in a pair of leather boxing gloves I found in a carton of shoes. No matter how tightly she tied them, the gloves slipped off my thin wrists as I danced about the yard punching at shadows and the wind.

      I remember kneeling as Nana raked piles of freshly cut grass into my open arms. Each inhale filled me with a scent so cool and fresh that I wanted to swim in it. The damp aroma moistened my nose as I loaded the soft green embraces into shopping bags. My first sneeze always cued Nana to declare our task complete. Nana sat the bags across the backseat of the pale blue Rambler while I ran into the house to fetch Grandpa. We drove three in the frontseat, and I had to shout to be heard while the engine was running. I can still feel the tickle of deer lips on my palm, the happy chill that ran through me as I stood stiffly, arm extended, hand piled with grass, feeding baby deer at the Springfield Children's Zoo.

I remember the treasure chest she kept for me in the front closet. A cigar box filled with campaign buttons—I recognized a few of the names, but most boasted the names of Republicans who won or lost local elections. Keys to undiscovered doors, tokens from a World's Fair, and an arrowhead Grandpa found in Yellowstone. Each visit, I would dig into the closet beneath the heavy coats and see what new items appeared in my private vault. One week a change purse from the Indy 500. The next, a pair of sunglasses.

I don't remember when her shoulders began to sag, but I remember realizing I was taller than Nana.

On my first visit to see her in the hospital, Mom and Dad warned me that she looked thin, that she was hooked to a machine, that her heart was still weak. I wanted to scream at the nurses "This is not my grandmother! Where is she? What have you done with Nana?"

I remember her ordering the medical staff around with Welsh commands. No one understood. Doctors, nurses, and interns carried out duties as I sat beside Nana pretending that I could translate for her, relaying meal requests. I remember feeling I'd let her down when all the Welsh I could give was a children's rhyme about a brave red dragon and a ballad of the shepherd girl longing for her sweetheart lost at sea.

When I drove my grandfather to the nursing home where she was recovering, he would hold her hand all afternoon, nodding in silent agreement as she scolded him for not wearing a hat, not ironing his pants, not taking her home.

I remember the intercom's buzz in the middle of an English test. My teacher looked my way, hung up the phone and

56

sent me to the office. The secretary told me to call home. I thought to myself: "Nana's dead," and, as I dialed, I tried to distinguish between a premonition and a wish. "Just because you felt it, you didn't cause it or want it to happen," I told myself over and over.

I remember my father crying at the funeral. I'd never seen him cry before. I've never seen him cry since.

I remember showing him a locket as we cleared out my grandmother's attic. "Whose hair is this?" I asked.

In a quiet voice he told me of Nana's only daughter: "I was seven when my baby sister Annie died of whooping cough."

I remember feeling an emptiness as big and hollow as all there was about my Nana I would never know, and then the fullness of how much of her would be remembered for a lifetime.

What Grandpa Saw

Every Fourth of July
between the parade and the fireworks,
Grandpa snuck us down to the cabinet
leaving Mom and Dad upstairs with Nana.
Filed away in the pine chest he built,
those guns were the only inheritance
Grandpa wanted to live
to see passed on.

Even the heaviest rifle looked light
in Grandpa's twisted claws.
He shared the history of each weapon
as if we were writing it down.
The flint-and-steel that smoked
in patriot hands at Bunker Hill,
the breechloader of a fur-trading scruff
who brought our French name via Canada.

Grandpa taught my brother and me
to clean and load each one.
"To aim a gun right," he said,
"you gotta see inside your mark."
Before racking the rifles
Grandpa slowly raised each weapon to his cheek,
winking his soul at some invisible target
in the corner.

Standing in a stillness
he could not achieve
after placing the gun in my brother's hold,
Grandpa tutored us
in this rite, ordered by age.
It would have been easier to ask

what Grandpa prayed
than what he saw through those sights.

When the tour of weapons was complete,
Grandpa turned back to the cabinet
and emerged with arms out to us,
a gun clenched in each knotted fist:
"You rack this rifle
like it's your own,
because it is."
And we did.

Outlasting Nana,
Grandpa moved in with us.
When he started slipping
he wore his belt as a tie,
brushed his teeth with the tube,
left us midsentence,
paused at every door
unsure if headed out or in.

Grandpa never offered the same gun twice.
He never confused
what he'd given my brother
with what he'd given to me.
Without ever pulling a trigger,
Grandpa taught me exactly
how to see inside my mark.

Dining with Lions

Have you ever watched lions dine?
The male waits impatiently
While his harem brings home the meat.
He eats intensely, undisturbed,
Indifferent to a visitor's inquiring eye.
He eats and eats till belly is past full.
Puffed with satisfied swell, he waddles away
For the nearest shade.
Stretched beneath a tree,
The lion oversees his pride
From a distance.

When they see that Lord Lion
Has licked his last chop,
The huntresses turn attention from tending cubs,
As they gather to enjoy their harvest,
Try to imagine the silent grace
Of their patient tracking,
The quick flurry of their violent assault.
After the shared effort of a hunt,
Doesn't it seem right that lionesses feast together?
They make room for their cubs beside them,
And table manners are playful.

If Daddy desires more,
They all step aside
And wait.

Watching lions dine,
You too may find yourself
Feeling quite at home.

Switch Hitting

Lefty or righty,
Every twitter and twitch,
Each adjustment of the jock strap,
The fingers wrapping the grip,
The balance, the stance, the swings,
We studied the postures of major leaguers.
My brother and I stood baseball cards
In proper batting order against a curb
In a town thirty miles from Fenway Park.

We played the game with passionate precision.
"Invisible man on second."
Announcing, umpiring, pitching and batting.
"Two down, bottom of the fifth,
Boston up by three."
I could never be the Red Sox
Because my brother was my brother
And I was his sister.
"You're lucky I let you play at all."

Tongue wadded in my own cheek,
I was Thurman Munson of the Yankees.
My brother made it clear,
In Cowboys-and-Indians, I was the Indians.
If he was the Americans, I was the V.C.
I had the homerun cut of Reggie Jackson
And every pinstriped pitcher's motion,
But my heart was with Boston and my hometown heroes.

I knew how Yaz leered over his left shoulder
And circled one wrist three times with the bat.
How Rico Petrocelli knocked dust from his cleats
And cocked his head at the pitcher,
Which cheek chipmunked tobacco

As Fisk dug his feet into dirt
And stiffly leaned over the plate.
"Can I be the Red Sox today?" I'd ask.
"No, you're the Yankees or we're not playing."

I never questioned my brother's calls—
Except when I was Billy Martin.
I'd throw my arms up,
Thrust out my chest,
Spit cuss words at the ump,
And kick the ground.
I used to wonder why it felt so good
To watch all the dust settling
On my brother's feet.

Sister Lucinda Taught Math

Sister Lucinda taught math
and coached our field hockey team.
She wore red high-top sneakers
and made me wish I was Catholic.

She invented playful rhymes to help
us remember the Pythagorean theorem
and sang silly songs as we ran laps
around the field before practice.

Sister Lucinda told us stories
of painters and Africa and zen buddhism
as if she carried them all
in the green backpack that hung on her shoulder.

I never could say when or where I heard
that Sister Lucinda had a baby
before she became a nun,
but everyone knew it to be true.

I'd beg Saturday night invitations
from my friend Margaret O'Leary
so I could go to St. Ann's
with her family on Sunday morning.

I would watch Sister Lucinda
kneeling, bowing her head, singing.
She looked so solemn and prayerful
that I couldn't help wondering if she

was remembering the child she lost
or gave up for adoption or hid away
in her closet. But even then I saw
the glow of love and joy in her face.

Even in her seriousness
Sister Lucinda looked at peace with God.
She and Sister Maryellen shared secrets during sermons—
with whispers, with glances, with smiles.

They marched around doing nun-like duties,
humming Latin and carrying candles.
Margaret O'Leary told me they organized
folk masses, and Mrs. O'Leary said

"It's a disgrace the way those two carry on."
At first I thought she was talking
about Margaret and me, but when Mr. O'Leary said
"Father Carpenter shouldn't let them teach the kids"

I thought Sister Lucinda was under attack
for sneakers, smiles and folk songs.
So I sat silent in the backseat
till the O'Learys dropped me at home.

In my room I cried and prayed
for Sisters Lucinda and Maryellen
knowing they had brought me closer to God
than Mr. and Mrs. O'Leary ever had.

A Child's Logic

I have known all my life
about God.
First I had words:
Father, Zeus, God, Jesus, Jehovah, Almighty.
Then images of robed men with beards,
and warriors, judges, priests.
I let go of the pictures
and words
and put my faith in the power
of love.

I have known all my life
about love.
First, no words,
only a crush on my softball coach,
and the wish to marry my best friend.
Child's logic told me
I wanted to be a boy
when all I wanted was to love
and be loved
by girls.

Then I heard secret words
that crowded out
what I felt
for my coach
and best friend.
Words so ugly
they couldn't describe
what beauty I felt.
Contradictions too great
to transcend,
and when they told me

God is love,
I saw Him
frowning
at me.

Coaxing My Uterus

at the time of her menstruation,
she shall be unclean.—Leviticus 12:2

I massage my belly
with desperate hopes of
coaxing my uterus
back on cycle

Curse the moon
for uncertainty
Curse the heavens
for fear
Zig-zag from toilet
to toilet
eager for any
evidence of
tell-tale spotting
red drops on the crotch
of underwear

Why so late?

I massage my belly
with desperate hopes of
coaxing my uterus
back on track

Check the calendar again
maybe it's a miscount
this month
But no—
already eight days late

I wait
afraid
and unclean

I massage my belly
with desperate hope

Charting Progress

My first year at college, I said no to desserts, hoping
to avoid the freshman ten everyone talked about.
I took up jogging and found I could actually
drop about a pound a week. Compliments
from friends and family made me want
a bathroom scale so I could chart my
progress. I weighed myself once
a week and felt giddy when I
could record a loss. Others
envied my control. Was
lighter than ever and
bought new clothes.
Stopped eating red
meat. Did sit-ups
every day. New
clothes grew
baggy. Ate
vegetables.
Felt giddy
Beautiful
Lettuce
no fat
bones

Anorexic's Profile

Like a soldier who buffs tarnish
from bars marking rank and
cleans bright each stripe
earned in battle,
I polish my ribs
one at a time
until each
shines
like
new.

This Beautiful

Flesh first falls from
breasts
then from my behind.
Next from hips and arms.
Eventually, wrists and fingers
thin out and old jewelry
slides in new ways.
Feet slip in shoes,
and hats grow too big
for my skull.
At last,
my eyes
sink
into
my
face
and my
sockets expand,
the only part
that isn't shrinking.

I chisel away at the
surface.
I discover a thrill
with each new
layer of
surface.
Lines of my thighs
fill with shadow
when I walk.
Sinews on my arm
dance when I squeeze.
When I breathe in,

skin pulls tight
against torso
and rib.

I always knew it was here—
this beautiful—though I
never thought it
would be so
easy to
see.

Fasting

a light-
headed dizzy
and dazzling
like crossing
the finish
line not
knowing if
you've won
or lost
not sure
if what
you feel
is pain
or joy—
what angels
must feel
when they
race God.
I consume
only wind
and water,
having cut
away flesh
of excess
and want.
No fear
of temptation.
No need
so great
it cannot
be met
by air.
On an
angel's diet

I share
every bite
I do
not take
with saints
who have
gorged on
God's will.

Promises to Myself

No desserts
Weigh in daily
No red meat
No chocolate
Eat lefty
Chew slowly
No bread
No dairy
No eggs
Chopsticks
Keep a calendar of what you eat
Sit-ups every morning
Run three times a week
No breakfast
No snacking
Push-ups for lunch
No letting big meals get absorbed
Run to the bathroom to throw up
Run the sink so no one hears
Stop being so regimented
Get control over this eating thing
Stop making lists

Answers to Nobody's Prayers

Today, in Buenos Aires,
a poodle plummeted thirteen stories,
killed a passerby,
and littered the sidewalk.
An onlooker stared so blindly
that she never saw the bus
that struck her dead.
As luck would have it,
before the medics arrived,
a middle-aged man collapsed
with heart failure:
a total of four lives lost.

Choices

I never chose birth,
but I choose
again and again
by the minute
the day
the hour
the moment
to live

Today
I am choosing
not to take
my life
and you
are choosing not
to take yours

Let's celebrate
together

Hotshot

A five-foot-eight-inch fifth grader is probably going to be one of the best basketball players in her school no matter if she's girl or boy. But I happen to be a girl, and pretty good at sticking the "J" too, so don't go challenging me to one-on-one, unless, of course, you don't mind losing. And I'm not gonna play you easy on account of what Mom calls "ego"—especially no "male ego" that some boys got. I don't play easy for any reason or anyone. It's that simple.

Most of life is simple. Too many people want to make stuff way more difficult than it is. Like the time school pictures came back and I was holding a pencil behind Tony Kramer's head so it looked like the pencil grew right out of his ear. Well, Mrs. Kramer goes and calls my teacher and then my Mom and we all have to sit down and discuss it. They all try to tell me what a horrible thing I did, messing up the picture and all. And I kept trying to tell them how funny it was—and even Tony thought so too—but no one else was laughing. So I end up feeling bad about something I thought was fun—and I would never have done it to someone like Laurie Strandy or Darius Silvers because I know it would have made them feel bad. But Tony—I knew he could take it.

Oh, well, I guess I'm supposed to be learning the when's and where's of having fun. And what I like most is fun on the basketball court. Shooting, dribbling, rebounding—I can out-run and out-jump anyone in the fifth or sixth grade—anyone!

Most of the teachers gave up on trying to make me stay on the girls' side of the hardtop. But old Miss Monzelli, who I call Miss Von Smelly when she can't hear me, sometimes still screeches from behind those pointy glasses with the fake little diamonds for me to get onto the hopscotch side of the blacktop. She says I can't play with the boys because it ain't ladylike. She

78

says I might get hurt. She also says that saying *ain't* ain't ladylike neither, so I do it just to remind her who's boss. We'll see who's going to get hurt.

Truth is, no boy ever hurt me more than I hurt him. Besides, I've had stitches four different times, and not once have I even cried at the blood or the needles. Broke a bundle of bones, too—three fingers, my wrist, both collarbones, and my left ankle—seven all together.

That's how I learned that basketball is in me—it's in my bones. Every time I've been sidelined, I don't mind missing out on a football game, or the roller coaster at the carnival, but not being able to play hoops sets my skin crawling. I know it's in my blood too because my Dad is six-foot-four and played in college. He still plays at the Y, and I get to shoot around at half-time of his games. All the referees there like me. Sure, they have to show off, spinning the ball on their fingers or throwing it to me behind the back, but they all like me. I figure they are jealous of the guys like Dad who get to strut their stuff while they only get to run up and down the court blowing whistles and ticking everyone off.

But at halftime, the refs rebound for me and call me Hotshot.

I'm telling you all this so you can see how some things are born in a girl even though most people seem to think they're reserved only for boys. And don't go calling me Tomboy unless you can give account of what it means. I'm a girl who can throw a football further and with a better spiral than anyone at Maple Street School, except for Greg Merrit, who is my best friend and Mr. Leon, the gym teacher. I don't mind that Greg can throw further than me because he's real good and that's just that. I can respect that. Besides, I'm a better free throw shooter than he is, so really, we're even. But don't go saying that I throw like a boy any quicker than you'd say that Greg throws like a girl, which he does, because he throws like me, and I'm a girl. There's nothing

79

Tomboy about it. I'm a girl and I can play a wizard game of Horse, I'm unbeatable at 'Round the World, I hold my own in 21 and you'll want me on your side if we're playing five-on-a-side pickup. I told you, it's that simple.

And I'm not good just because I'm tall. My Dad told me not to be worried about being a six-foot girl because he says if any girl is going to dunk in high school it's going to be me. Mom says I slouch too much. I don't think I slouch at all. I just lean kind of forward when I walk and bounce on my toes so I can feel my hightops hugging my ankles. Air Hotshot! I hit the ground and my treads spring me right back up on my toes. I can see that it scares the boys a bit when I stride out onto the court bouncing like I'm the best thing since the hook shot in my black leather Cons. I'll take hightops over high heels any day!

Anyhow, what I'm trying to tell you about is my problem with Miss Monzelli. She's my Social Studies teacher who seems to think she got hired by the school solely to mess with my life. She tries to make me play only with the other girls at recess, and I told her I don't have anything against girls, but I like playing basketball, and it's the boys who play basketball. She says I'm not learning to be a lady if I don't play with girls and held me after school to point out that if I dress like the boys and talk like the boys, I'll find myself in trouble. It seemed to me that the only trouble I was in was with her, but I didn't think I'd score points by telling her so. Instead, I asked her if it was bad for me to be like the boys, why wasn't it bad for the boys to be like boys. After all, I didn't see her making no fuss about what they were wearing or playing.

Miss Monzelli got all red in the face so that her cheeks and neck matched the fire-engine-red lipstick she wears. She chewed me out for being fresh, and then insisted that the boys are supposed to act like boys because they are boys. It didn't make sense to me, so I didn't listen to most of what she was saying until I caught on that she had phoned my Mom to say that I was supposed to wear dresses to school unless we were scheduled

80

for gym class. Well, we only have gym twice a week, so Miss Von Smelly was saying that I had to wear a dress every Monday, Wednesday, and Friday! Now, I don't even like wearing dresses when I go to see my grandmother in the city, but that's the deal. And even then I don't like it, but my grandmother does. Gram is worth pleasing for the way she lets me climb on through the attic to the roof. Gram keeps a treasure chest for me in the closet and takes me to the zoo. Her oatmeal cookies are the best on this planet, and I get to lick the batter from the bowl. She even sewed me a pair of pajamas with tiger stripes and a long tail stuffed with nylon stockings. For Gram I will wear a dress.

Mom gave up with me and dresses when I was in the third grade. That's when we agreed that I wouldn't fight over wearing a dress for Sunday mass or for visits to Gram. If I didn't put up a stink on those occasions, I wouldn't have to wear dresses the rest of the whole year. At Gram's house and God's house, it makes Mom happy if I wear a dress, but no way am I wearing no dress for no old Miss Von Smelly—not even if she could bake oatmeal cookies like Gram's. Mom's only other rule was "No hightop sneakers when wearing a dress!" I don't much mind that rule, because hightops just don't look right when you got a skirt flapping around your thighs.

Mom lets me wear low-cut sneakers with my knee socks, so I can still run around, because I wear shorts underneath. I just don't like the idea that when I sprint, jump, fall or wrestle the whole world has a front-row seat to my underwear. And if I wear a dress to school, I have to put up with all Miss Von Smelly's stupid comments to us girls to sit with our knees locked together so our legs get all sore and cramped from trying to keep ourselves all shut up tight under our desks, as if it isn't easier to just tell the boys they got no business looking up our skirts in the first place.

I've never seen Miss Von Smelly in pants, and I feel like telling her how much happier she'd be if she didn't have to pay so much worrytime making sure her underwear ain't on display when she bends over, or reaches up high, or just stands in the wind. She wears all these silly shoes that make her look like a Barbie doll when she walks—stiff-kneed and pointy-toed, scuttering along.

I don't understand Miss Monzelli any better than she understands me, but I don't go telling her that she should be wearing hightop sneakers and jeans, so where does she get off calling my Mom to say that I have to dress like her? That's all I want to know.

So anyway, I go home, and at dinner, Mom tells Dad about Miss Monzelli's phone call, and I just about choke on a tomato when Dad says "If that's what the teacher says, I suppose Angela will just have to put up with the rule."

"But Dad, Miss Monzelli is such a witch. She's just making me wear dresses because she knows how much I hate it! She's out to get me!"

"Now, Tiger," Dad calls me "Tiger" when we horse around or when he wants me to think that he's on my side, but he's really not. "I'm sure Miss Monzelli is not out to get you. She is your teacher, and she knows what is best for you and for the school."

"I'm not wearing dresses three times a week!"

"Honey," Mom calls me that when I start getting stubborn, and I can tell it's going to be two against one, three against one if you count Miss Monzelli. "I've let you take responsibility for your wardrobe this year, but maybe it's time that we take another look at what is appropriate attire for a young lady in your school. What do the other girls wear?"

"Mom," I could hear the whine in my voice, which meant that I knew reasoning wouldn't really work, "the other girls in my school play hopscotch at recess, and go to the corner store for Doritos and Coke after school. They don't play basketball or football or even climb on the jungle gym."

82

"Well, you could come home and change into your play clothes after school if you wanted to . . ."

"Aww, come on, Mom, I'd never get in the game if I came home while the kids were choosing up teams. Dad . . ." I looked hopefully to my father for support, but he was staying out of this argument for as long as possible.

"Angela," my father said with a mix of sympathy and hesitation in his voice, "your teacher seems to think . . ."

"Dad, my teacher is a witch who waddles around in high heels and can't even hold a football in one hand. She picks it up at arm's length with two hands, like it's a piece of corn on the cob, too hot to bring within three feet of her body."

"Now, that's no way to talk about your teacher."

"Then there's no way she should talk about me as if I have no right to dress as I please."

Both my parents seemed to be defending Miss Monzelli only because she was my teacher, but I could tell that words were not going to convince them of what a jerk Miss Monzelli was being. So I sat quiet, hoping they would just forget about it, and life would go on as usual as I trotted off to school in my hightops and jeans the next morning. Besides, I didn't even own enough dresses to get through a week without repeating, unless I wore the satin dress I had from being the flower girl at my cousin's wedding. That dress puffed out so that I looked like a piece of Double Bubble Chewing Gum wrapped up and twisted in bows at both ends. No way was I stepping out of the house in that thing!

My other two dresses had both been made by Gram. My favorite was yellow with purple and white stripes down the side and a big number 32 on the front. Gram made it special to look like Magic Johnson's Lakers uniform. For a dress, it's pretty neat, but it's still a dress. None of the other dresses I own fit me because I've been growing too fast for my clothes to keep up with me. The only reason the gum-wrapper dress fits is because an older cousin was supposed to be the flower girl, but she got some mono-disease right before the wedding, and I had to take her place. The dress was too big in the first place.

So Mom and Dad go on as if this conversation is over. I dig into my fish stick as if there's something special about fish sticks, which there definitely is not. I hear my fork scratching my plate, Mom's bracelets knocking against each other, and Dad's jaw cracking the way that it does when he chews. In our family, that's a silent dinner table.

When Mom gets up to clear the table, I leap up to help because I don't want anyone pointing out how much I hate all this housework stuff as if it's because I don't wear dresses often enough. Besides, it helps change the tone of everything for dessert, and we have forgotten the whole conversation enough so that Dad pulls out the weekend football pool that he gets at work. It's the first round of the playoffs, and I'm still hopeful enough to believe that I can bet on the Patriots to make it to the Super Bowl. Dad says that his football sense overrules his loyalty to the hometeam, so he plays his card differently than I play mine. We argue a bit about whether or not the Patriots can get their ground game going, and then we turn attention to the chocolate pudding Mom puts in front of us. The silence is broken, and when I go to bed I feel sure no one will notice what I wear to school in the morning.

☆　　☆　　☆　　☆　　☆

"Do you have Phys Ed today?" Mom asks as I throw my backpack full of books on the kitchen floor by the backdoor.

"Umm, no. Why?" I pretend innocence and ignorance of Miss Monzelli's mandate.

"Well, because, we agreed that you'd save your jeans for gym days." Mom's trying to be as forgetful of the argument as I am.

"We agreed that I could wear whatever I wanted except for church and for Gram. We never agreed to anything about wearing dresses to school. Miss Von Smelly just poked her nose into something that is not her business." Since this was not one of those times when giving in for the sake of keeping Mom happy was worth it, I made sure not to say *ain't*. I didn't want her to have any dirt on me in any way. Otherwise, I'd be stuck for good. I hoped she'd see this as one of those times when giving in for the sake of keeping ME happy would be worth HER while.

It wasn't.

"Angie, the school has its expectations and standards, and you have to . . ."

"Mom, it's not the school. It's Miss Monzelli! And she's an old witch anyway. Why listen to her?"

Dad walked in and silence returned.

I grew impatient and started pleading. "Mom, watch, No one will say anything's wrong if you just let me keep doing what I'm doing."

"Oh-oh, dresses again, huh? Tiger, why don't you just put on a dress, go to school, and do whatever it is you always do?" offered Dad, trying to be helpful and healing to the conversation.

"Daaadddd," I whined, hoping the tone said more than the word itself.

"Tiger, no one is asking you to change yourself. Nobody is going to stop you from being who you are. It's only your clothes we're asking you to change."

"Well, if it's only clothes, then why is everyone else making such a gigantic deal about what I wear?"

For a moment I grew hopeful when my Dad had no answer for me, but then Mom filled the pause. "Because your teacher thinks you ought to dress up a bit more—like the other girls."

"Exactly," seconded Dad. "So why don't you run back into your room, slip those clothes into your backpack for after school, and put on a dress for classes?"

It was more of a commandment than a question, and I knew I wasn't going to get out of the house in my jeans. So I just glared at Dad a bit, then glared even harder at Mom, and stormed back to my room.

I had tried to be honest with my parents, but my honest opinions had gotten me nowhere. I didn't really want to cut school, although that option did come to mind. I figured I could change my clothes as soon as I got around the corner from the house. So, I put on the dress I hated most, the candy-wrapper one from Rico's wedding. It looked really stupid with my sneakers, and I felt like irking my folks because they were siding with Miss Von Smelly. I wore one tube sock with black and orange stripes and one with green and blue stripes, all of which completely clashed with the yellow and red of the dress.

I stomped my way back into the kitchen, no longer hungry for breakfast. I stood in the doorway as defiantly as possible with legs spread wide and arms folded across my chest. Mom and Dad looked at each other, unimpressed by me, and pleased as punch they'd won the argument. I stuffed my jeans and a T-shirt into my backpack as Dad had suggested, but I guess he must of been onto my plan to change before I reached the schoolyard because he offered to drive me to school.

86

Next thing I know, Dad's dropping me off in the school parking lot, and I'm facing a blacktop filled with my friends who have never even seen me in a dress, let alone in a flower girl gown, and I can't believe it. I'm angry as can be at Mom, Dad, Miss Monzelli, and any kid who dares to look at me. I turn to get back into the car, and when Dad innocently waves "So long, Tiger. See you tonight," I can't believe he's humiliating me this way. I see a few kids pointing toward me, laughing, and I want to punch them all. I don't know where to begin swinging, so I run inside to the girls' room, leap into the second stall, lock the door, and stand up on the seat so that no one can find me.

As I'm catching my breath, I discover that I left my backpack in the car.

Everybody has already seen me and I'm weighing my options while perched atop of the toilet. Then I hear the bathroom squeak open. By the clicking of tiny footsteps echoing across the tile, I know Miss Monzelli has stalked me down.

"Hello? Is anyone in here? Hello? Angela? Angela?"

I say nothing, but I think of how stupid I'll feel if she finds me hiding in the stall. I know she knows I'm in here. I quickly and quietly slide my feet down so that it looks like I'm sitting on the toilet, and I drop my underpants down around my ankles. "Yes, Miss Monzelli," in the sweetest voice I can put together. "I'm just, well, ya know, doing what I have to do."

"Oh, Angela, it's you," she says, as if she's surprised I'm here. "I saw someone sneak in, and you know you shouldn't leave the playground without permission. Unless of course it's an emergency. I suppose it's all right this one time if Nature caught you by surprise." She's trying to make me feel better, but it sure as cinnamon ain't working.

"By the way, I thought you looked very pretty when I saw your father drop you off."

That was the final straw. I wanted to scream, punch or puke at her. She sounded so smug in her triumph, like those TV preachers who have saved some stupid sinner from the clutches of the devil. But fighting Miss Von Smelly would be no solution. It would only help prove to her that I behaved unladlyike. So I said nothing, and she filled the silence by explaining that she was going back out before the bell rang to line everyone up for homeroom. Again, the bathroom door squeaked and the echoing heel clicks out the door and down the hallway.

I hated the thought of being made fool by Miss Monzelli's dumb rules. I needed a way to make her own rules work for me rather than against me. So I sat for a bit, realizing I might as well pee while I was on the toilet seat. After finishing my piss, I stood and reached to pull my underwear back up. As I turned to flush, a comic vision flashed through my head. I quickly dropped my underwear back to my ankles and stepped out of one leg hole. With my other leg, I kicked it up into the air, then with one arm I reached out to first catch and then slam dunk my underwear into the toilet bowl. A quick kick to the metal bar flushed it all away. No more underwear!

Miss Monzelli could gloat all she wanted over her little victory because I knew I'd have the last laugh. I wasn't thrilled about the razzing I'd have to put up with in the meantime, but it would all be worthwhile.

I returned to the blacktop where everyone was lining up silent and military. Eyes flashed my way, and an occasional head turned, but always at the risk of Miss Monzelli taking away recess period for headturners to practice standing at attention. I always wondered what it was we were supposed to pay attention to.

I held my head high and looked at no one. I had a secret that would teach Miss Monzelli not to mess with my life or my wardrobe so I figured I didn't have to deal with any kid's questions or stares. I just strutted to my place in the back of the line, glad that my last name was Vickery so I was at the end of the alphabetical order that Miss Monzelli organizes her life by. I glared down at Eric Tydings who stood in front of me every time we lined up for anything. He turned with a giggle held under his breath, and I answered his jeering. "If you don't turn around and get rid of that jackass grin, I'm gonna make your teeth permanent fixtures in your stomach."

Eric quickly turned back to the front, and it was a good thing for him, because the line was filing into the school, and Miss Monzelli for sure would have slapped him with some detention time for not paying attention. And no way was she going to blame me for his mischief today. After all, I was wearing a dress, and in Miss Monzelli's book, girls in dresses act ladylike and stay out of trouble.

I spoke to no one all morning except to answer questions with "yes" or "no," because I had nothing much I wanted to say to anyone. We had lots of stuff to do, including a worksheet of word problems, some reading about astronauts, and a spelling test. I pretended not to notice all the attention I was getting—the muffled laughter, stolen glances and flat-out stares—but inside I wasn't missing a single sidelook or whisper. All the while I sat real careful not to let on that I wore nothing beneath my dress. I wanted to be sure that Miss Monzelli could not get word that I had no underwear on. I was determined that the whole school should see for themselves all at the same time, so I waited patiently for morning recess.

The recess bell finally rang at 10:30 just as I was completing an essay about my favorite animal. I had written all that I could think of writing about kangaroos about five minutes earlier, but I added one final sentence to my essay before putting up my pencil and folding my hands together on my desk top the way Miss Monzelli insists we all sit before she will consider allowing us to line up for recess. I wrote, "Kangaroos prove God has a sense of humor, because the only reason kangaroos exist is to jump around and have fun."

I signed my essay the way I always do at the end. Miss Monzelli hates it because she wants my name squished up at the top right corner of the page, neatly printed with her name and the date. She insists we use the "proper heading" on our work, so I do that, but I also let loose in big script letters at the end "by Angela Vickery" like a painter signing a masterpiece.

"All right, children. You may line up quietly in alphabetical order if you would like to go outside for recess." Of course everyone wanted to go out for recess, but Miss Monzelli always made it sound like an option and an invitation all at the same time that it was really, deep down, just another Von Smelly command.

We lined up, with me in the back again, and filed silently down the corridor to the double doors that lead to the playground. Once outside we were allowed to break file, and we scattered ourselves across the blacktop. Kevin Marino was close on my heels asking, "Hey, Angela. What's with the dress?" and I was answering only with an all-out sprint to the basketball court. Tyrone Freeman had the ball, and he was staring a game of "21" rather than choosing up sides for full court. Recess was too short for a game, and "21" gave everyone a chance to play because it's one big half-court game that leaves everyone against everyone scrapping to make a basket. You just have to keep track of your own score, and it's you against everyone any time you get the ball.

So I threw out my elbows the way I always did and made space for myself in the middle of the crowd huddled below the basket. The boys knew me well enough to tell from the scowl on my face that questions or jokes were completely out of order, so we all just settled in to play basketball. When Tyrone missed an outside shot, the rebound went off my fingers, and Stu Jackster came up with the ball. He cleared the ball out past the foul line, and I went out with him to play defense. He drove to my left, but his leg caught my knee, and we both went to the pavement. I landed sitting flat on my fanny with Stu sprawling across my legs. My dress was all in place, and Stu spit at the

90

pavement beside me as he extended a hand to help me up. Meanwhile, the ball had gotten loose, and Greg Merrit had scored on a jump shot.

Greg got to take the ball up top because it's "make it–take it" where you get the ball back after you score a hoop. As Greg went to take a shot from the top of the key, I went back under to rebound. Sure enough, I came up with the ball, and put it straight up for a point of my own. It was my ball, at the top, and I took the ball left, spun around back to the right, and after two dribbles, I put the ball up and off the backboard for another basket.

My ball again. This time Tyrone decides to play me close, and as I move to spin past him, he gets help on the double team from Greg Merrit. BANG! Greg and I collide, and this time I'm on my back with my hightop sneakers looking down at me. Tyrone screams, "She's got no underwear on!" and they're all laughing hysterically. I clench my teeth almost as tightly as my fists and hiss out at them with squinted eyes "Miss Monzelli says I gotta wear a dress. Man, I'm wearing a dress, aren't I? You laugh at her, not at me, Tyrone Freeman. If any of you wanna laugh at me, you gonna have all your faces rearranged!"

Tyrone backed down on account we're friends, but Doug McDermott wasn't so smart. He starts chanting "I see London. I see France. Angela got no underpants." Once Doug gets going, everyone joins him, and I go right for his throat. He lands a half-punch the side of my head, and I throw one he ducks away from. Next thing I know, we're rolling around on the court, neither one of us landing any punches, but my dress is caught up high and my naked butt must be mooning the whole world just as Miss Monzelli arrives at the fight. Her voice is an extra two octaves higher than usual when I hear her scream "Angela Vickery, stop it! Stop this instant. Stop!"

Of course, I'm not stopping. I'm barely listening, but she tells one of the kids to run and get Mr. Stoller, the school principal.

Well, lots of fussing went on about this whole scene. The kids loved it. It was a scandal that had teachers and the principal unsure about what to do. After all, they had brought it on themselves. As Greg Merrit said, "You ask Angie to wear a dress and you gotta expect something crazy!"

Mr. Stoller lectured me a long while about fighting, but he never said anything directly about my lack of underwear. The school nurse gave me a whole lot of nurse-like advice about being clean and wearing the proper undergarments. My Mom and Dad had a conference that afternoon with Miss Monzelli, but didn't say much to me about it.

The next day, when I arrived at breakfast in jeans and a Lakers sweatshirt, Mom asked if I wanted Wheaties or Grapenuts and that was that. Even after all the dust settled, Miss Monzelli never brought up the subject of dresses or underwear.

When the weekend arrived, Mom announced that Gram had invited us to the city for the day. I ran back upstairs to my room and happily put on my Magic Johnson dress. When I returned to the kitchen for breakfast, Mom and Dad looked at me, and then at each other, relieved.

I answered their unasked question by quickly turning, bending and lifting my skirt to show them my underwear.

"Looking good, Tiger!" cheered Dad as I turned around to face my smiling parents.

"What are you waiting for? Go on, get dressed. I want to sink my teeth into Gram's oatmeal cookies while they're still warm."

III.
Relationships
Blossom

When the Women Huddle

Seated amid the unmarrieds,
I hold back from conversation,
Drink only seltzer,
And turn away from hors d'oeuvres.
I pick at the banquet
As if to assure myself a reason
For feeling empty
When this reception ends.

A cousin of the groom
Locks eyes with me
Every time our glasses
Kiss a toast,
And I steal
Secret glances to
Invite further offers
Of champagne.

While others pair off
To dance
We remain seated
Dabbling in cake too sweet,
Giggling over low necklines,
Emptying another bottle,
And I cannot get
My fill.

Legs brush, unseen,
Beneath table
And linger.
Nylon stocking clings
To nylon stocking.
I blush in confusion:

Was that my lead
Or is her leg seeking mine?

When the women huddle
For the tossing of flowers,
We stand together
At the outer edge of expectation,
On the fringe of female hope,
And when the bride delivers the bouquet our way,
We let it fall
Between.

New Year's Resolution

I have eaten enough all evening for a month,
And I fear a hangover that might last forever.
I should cart myself home,
But I hear myself suggesting coffee,
A bite to eat,
An all-night diner.
My eyes feasting on hers,
Brown the color of chestnuts
I hoarded in childhood pockets,
Pretending to store for use
In a neighborhood fracas,
When all I wanted was to keep them near,
Guaranteeing myself a bit of smooth
In a rough world.
And here I sit
Wanting to keep her near
Perhaps I am still pretending.
But my ears thirst for whispers
Of her breath.
I dream her skin on mine.
Hers as dark as mine is light,
Hers as rich and warm as the coffee
Placed before us
And when she pours cream
Into her cup
Brown and white
Dance in curls
That swirl evenly,
In defiance of separation.
She lifts the mix
To her lips,
And I dream her skin
On mine,
Her breath

On my breath.
I am more drunk now
Than I have been all evening
Here in the New Year's afterbirth.
I can no longer tell
What I think,
Or what she thinks,
But she is with me still,
And each swallow
Goes down so smoothly.

Dreaming

Dreamt gay last night.
Thousands of women embraced.
Fingertips braided to fingertips,
Thighs threading thighs,
Women laced together,
Linking limbs, joining lips and
Riding the hips of one another,
Women woven into a world
Where the only colors that matter
Are the rainbow,
Where lavender flames
Flow through pink valleys
Under an amethyst moon,
And white rivers run warm
With the milk of mothers whose wombs
Are seeded by the wind.

Dreamt gay last night.
Saw my own reflection
In crystal eyes
Of a woman riding the moon.
Bathed myself in the lap
Of a woman whose shadow
Was a mountain and
Whose breath was the wind.
I danced to the laughter and love
Of women singing themselves into
The lives of one another:
Tender women, fiery women,
Gentle and strong women
Daring women and loving women
Glowing at the touch
Of other loving women.

Dreamt gay last night.
And if I'm lucky
I will again
Tonight.

First Kiss

I don't know how I imagined it might be
Perhaps uncomfortable, like new shoes,
Or dry and bitter like a stale rye bread,
But your woman's kiss was full and warm and silky wet.
When your tongue met the wall of my teeth,
It patiently swam inside my lower lip before
Gently slipping through a hypnotized jaw.
Visions of angry Bible wavers,
Recalled childhood notions of wrong,
And vague memories of hushed whispers
About my unmarried uncle.
But soon I could think of nothing but your tongue.
As it played a symphony inside my mouth
On the ivory keys of my jaw.

And when your hands started exploring
In harmony with your kiss
My own hands began to move with the music.
My fingertips found yours and then
My palms moved up your long, firm arms
Finding smooth round shoulders,
And then following your collar bone
To the discovery that your chest heaved hot
At that moment I felt your fingers
Slide into a wetness I could not have controlled
Even if I had tried.

I don't know how I imagined it might be
Perhaps uncomfortable, like new shoes,
Or dry and bitter like a stale rye bread,
But your woman's kiss was full and warm and silky wet.

New World

Lifting my head to look across my world to yours,
I see that we have created a universe of our own.
Eye to eye, we have between us
an ocean of sweat with soft waves lapping up
to the shores of my breasts.
My sigh, a tropical zephyr that tickles beach grasses,
bends palm trees and molds sand to dunes
never shaped before.

Our bodies—the continents
bridging the waters of the world.
Our hands—the clouds sailing the globe,
touching but never resting
on the earth's surface.

In bed, together,
we are the
universe.

Earthquakes and tremors,
lightning and rainbows move only
with our strokes and trembles.
As you lick in salty froth of ecstasy.
I want to touch my tongue to yours,
and you can read it in my reach.
So, you move to me, climbing like the first life-form,
emerging from primordial womb and wet.
You slide your sweetness and sweat
against my own rising chest
and we breathe life into one another.
We lap up kisses that drop from waterfalls
and spring from volcanos.
I can taste the sea warmth
on your breath as you lean

over me, and my tongue
finds its way down the mountainside that is
your neck, your shoulder, your breasts, your torso.

Rocking the mesas, we are canyons, mountain ridges,
peaks and valleys, rivers and rainfall.
We are granite, snowflakes, and spider webs.
Rolling ourselves, we spin silky softness,
building cocoons of unearthly intimacy.
My body is weightless as I wrap myself
around, on top and inside of you.
We touch and become one
in a cataclysmic moment
that gives birth to
a new world.

Hooked

a day between autumn color
and winter stillness
we go fishing.
attention turned
to baiting hooks and casting lines
no one mentions the breezy chill.
I watch you wrestle
a brook trout
teasing tugging finally hooking.
you reel in
send out slack
reel in again.
you rise from the granite shore
rod arched forward
body arched back,
but what I see
is you
torn in half
as you land the trout
my sympathies
are with the fish.
hard lines of concentration
melt into smile
as you triumphantly puppeteer
the dangling captive.
you delight in the iridescent scales
the final slap of fish tail
and the last flash of resistance.
you scoop the exhausted fish
up and out of the water
and pose with your prey
who hangs like a heavy half-moon
a crescent that will shrink away
a fallen leaf decaying in an abandoned well.

our eyes meet—
mine and the lidless fish eyes—
locked in unblinking exchange.
pinched grey fish mouth motioning soundless cries
serrated gills gasping in silent suffocation
unable to shut out vision
the eye bulges through the webbing
to tell me we are caught
in the same
net.

What's a Nice Girl Doing?

Do you come here often?
This is my first time.
What's a nice girl doing
In a place like this?

This is my first time.
My mother would die to see me
In a place like this.
But I had to see for myself.

My mother would die to see me
In the arms of another woman,
But I had to see for myself
Where life and fantasy meet.

In the arms of another woman
I feel my breath lifted.
Where life and fantasy meet:
The touch of her skin on mine.

I feel my breath lifted,
Nakedness turned inside out.
The touch of her skin on mine;
I cannot separate the two.

Nakedness turned inside out
By needs that race against time.
I cannot separate the two:
The need to hide and the need to be seen.

By needs that race against time,
I am overtaken.
The need to hide and the need to be seen
Disappear in the moment of her touch.

I am overtaken.
Fears dissolve,
Disappear in the moment of her touch.
Her warmth builds a home.

Fears dissolve
When one loves honestly.
Her warmth builds a home
I can always taste.

When one loves honestly,
Does it matter how and with whom?
I can always taste
If she's not being true to herself.

Does it matter how and with whom?
Do you come here often?
If she's not being true to herself,
What's a nice girl doing?

Thanksgiving

One roasting turkey,
two pumpkin pies
and three generations
gather for homecoming
and football.

Breakfast dishes washed and shelved
as the men pass around the morning paper
and the boys toss a football outside.
Only enough time for toothbrush
and last-minute details
before we load Uncle Henry's van
and head for the high school—
all the men, the boys, and I.
My mother no longer has to badger me
for whatever help she needs before I go.
Finally, I dash upstairs to throw a sweatshirt on.
To declare myself ready I grab my boots by the door,
wave to the women. The men are already settling into the
        van.
They took turns in the shower while I set the table,
Mom stirred oatmeal, and we chatted.
I have always been the only girl
or woman
to go to the game,
but that was never an excuse from kitchen duties.

At the game,
I engage in the discussion
of offensive strategy and defensive hustle
but in silence I try to ignore other analysis:
the strengths and weaknesses
of the cheerleaders' breasts.
Every year, Dad saves my sanity.

108

Today he defends the virtue of
"a quick sense of humor
and backspin on her jumpshot."
My cousins look confused,
but Dad looks my way and winks.
As I am wondering if he knows
I'm dating a point guard from Smith,
the boys go full force into the breast debate:
Small-and-firm or Full-and-bouncy?
Before I know what I'm saying
I chime in
"Less filling, tastes great."
My cousins look even more confused.

At home, I will add a leaf to the table
as my mother and grandmother unfold the tablecloth.
The three of us work together
spreading the giant linen,
and I try to dodge their questions
about men and marriage.
I can't stop hearing unspoken wishes
for me to mother-in the next generation.
We toss the tablecloth above our heads,
and a suspended moment hangs
above us with the linen.
I stand arms raised
as mother and grandmother widen eyes
at unshaven armpits.
Displeased surprise on their faces
and I feel naked, at first,
then somehow revealed.
But they cannot decipher
love for women
in two tangles of fur that disappear
as my arms return to my sides.

Gravity spreads the cloth
unevenly,

upon the table.
As the three of us reach in
to smooth it down,
Gram chews her bottom lip
in the same nervous fashion
I thought
I'd inherited from my mother.
All three of us are lip-chewing
and simultaneously we notice,
shaking with three generations of laughter.

That's when I also see
in my grandmother's eyes
the exact slant of light
that sparkles in a photograph of me
framed above my lover's desk.

The folds are erased from the table,
the cloth edges hang evenly on all sides.
The three of us lift our arms in a strong embrace
and no one cares about my wooly armpits.

Because They Are Mine

I am not a man
trapped in a woman's body,
but a woman held prisoner
in a world
expecting me to fit
into uncomfortable shoes
and walk with a certain swing of the hips
along roads that lead to alien pastures.
Call it perspiration or sweat,
but know that it is wet, just the same.
My glow is laced
with grit and grease
from the front axle.
It's my car,
so I fix it,
and then I fix
dinner
and wash the laundry,
happy to hang her sweaters and socks to dry.
When I have time,
I alternate her underwear on the line
with mine,
knowing that nobody cares but me.
I have only myself to please,
and I enjoy tinkering, creating, rebuilding.
I love the songs that spin from my bicycle
after I've freshly packed the bearings,
the melody my cat purrs when I stroke
the thick fur surrounding his ears.
I love the smell that kicks
when my chain saw chews pine
as much as a fresh cut of roses.
I rock with pleasure
at the silent rhythms my body finds

shoveling snow, walking in sand,
and breathing beside the woman I love.
I revel in the salty taste of sweat
hanging on my upper lip
when my work demands it.
All responses are womanly
because they are mine.
I have only myself to please,
and it pleases me to love her.

Late Harvest

Seeds bought with paper route money.
Fist-size holes carefully spaced
by the width of my first-grader's hand.
Kernels of promise tenderly placed
and packed in dark soil,
signed by my fingerprints.

A baseball thrown wild
within a stride of my
well-watered plot
and I was screaming
"That's my garden!"
and calling the culprit "Idiot" or "Creep."

I, who sided with the dog
whenever Mom admonished him
for muddying the couch
or shaking wet on the walls,
would kick and cuss at Rusty
if he peed near my crops.

By summer's end, I'd interrupt games
to strut my tiny strip of dirt,
pulling up on slender green sprouts
no more miraculous than grass,
but, holy cow,
there dangled

carrots—
the size and shape and color
of slugs.
I'd wash the dirt off
with my own spit
and munch away.

By the steam-spewing hose
growing up from the cellar,
a row of corn stalks pushed skyward.
Every day, I'd check for ears and measure:
according to my belt buckle,
then armpits, chin, and, finally, my nose.

But the stalks would not sprout
and my corn grew to be my burden.
Carrots no longer held my interest,
and every day my concern grew larger
as my chances of success with corn
grew slimmer and slimmer.

Back to school
erased gardens from my mind
until my teacher's stories of the Pilgrims
planted the idea in my head
that we had to have homegrown corn
for Thanksgiving.

I boasted to everyone
that my corn would be ready for our feast,
and I went back to my daily routine
of tending garden
and trusting in hard work
and Plymouth Rock.

My parents tried to keep my expectations low by
promising pumpkin pie and turkey
even if my corn chose not to grow.
But the second-grader I was
had no room for doubts,

and by mid-November,
despite an early snowfall,
my faith remained strong.

114

On the day before Thanksgiving,
school let out at noon
and still no corn.

Thanksgiving morning
and my mother sent us out
to play freeze tag in the backyard.
I heard a rap on the picture window,
and there was Mom pointing down
at my meager strip of stalks and weeds.

My corn!
Three ears on the ground.
Three more, huge and suspended
at unimagined angles
waiting to be plucked off their stalks
by my thankful, believer's hands.

Husking all six ears
turning them over and over
weighing them against one another
gathering the golden threads we called angel's hair
and running my fingers through the strands
the way I petted Rusty's collie tail.

Dancing the naked yellow spears
past every relative and back to the kitchen,
I placed them in the boiling kettle,
and it would be some twenty years
before I gave serious thought
to the source of my last-minute harvest.

Thanksgiving Day, twenty years later.
Someone's comment about the corn
sparks Mom to tell the tale
of sneaking store-bought ears
into creases of my fruitless stalks.
Laughter around the table.

My mouth hangs in amazed disappointment.
Mom says "I thought you knew."
A playful elbow pokes my ribs
and everyone shares laughter with
the woman I have brought
into the family.

By telling the story for my lover's sake,
my mother names her heir to our lore.
I marvel at the distance between moments:
Twenty Thanksgivings
have come and gone
since my mother made the miracle of corn.

Not so much time has passed,
but as much realization perhaps,
between this moment of surprise
and the time my mother's mouth hung
in amazed disappointment
when I said to her "I thought you knew."

Myths have worn out
their welcome.
We are more skeptical
where last-minute miracles are concerned,
but, as always, there is much
to be thankful for.

The Language of Bottles

A dayful of
work worries,
traffic hassles,
and separation from her
dissolves into a golden sunset in right field.
Then, victory beers at the VFW
even though we didn't win.

We buy by the round
and speak the language of bottles.
Raise them to praise a teammate,
Glass to glass contact marks friendship,
a thump on the table, exasperation or anger.
When Brenda complains about
"the kid's father," the thud on the table
sends all the empties wobbling.
Joanie points the long bottle neck of her Miller Lite
to keep my attention tuned to her troubles with her boss.
Darlene peels the label
and tries to joke about her mother's Alzheimer's.
Martha taps my Bud with hers
and the foam cascades into my lap
as she asks "So, where's your friend?"

Everyone lies a bit at the VFW—
about the umpire's calls,
about how many beers they've had,
about lovers.

We manage to laugh till midnight,
but like fairy-tale spells
that fashion glass slippers
and turn pumpkins to sedans,

117

the magic of the team
melts in the parking lot
as we stagger off to separate cars.

I stop at the all-night donut shop
where she and I used to pick up
breakfast on our way to work.
Mindlessly, I order two to go,
and when I return to my car,
there is no fairy godmother
to grant my wish.

Road Trips

Somewhere, between the Verrazano Bridge,
the speeding ticket you talked us out of,
the too many beers, your sarcastic humor,
my backseat driving, our cigarette smoke,
and the hangover that lasted two days,
enough of you smiled upon me.

My thirst grew for fewer beers
and more of you.

Sometimes, between the Plough 'N' Stars Pub,
the soggy onion rings, our impromptu sing-alongs,
the miniature golf we never played,
the frontseat undressing in midtown traffic,
the arm wrestling on your kitchen floor,
I knew I wanted to hug you past tomorrow.

Somehow, when we touched under the table,
leaned together on the counter waiting for tea,
shared the worst martini in Brooklyn,
traded secret glances in the museum,
indulged in everything except sleep,
I worried that I was only imagining.

Someway, between where you are now,
and where I want to be holding you forever,
I dream of writing love songs
that bring us back
to those thirsty sing-alongs and smiles
on the road trips of yesterday.

Flirtation

The wordless voice
of possibility.
The silent play
of light on water when
a tongue runs along a row of teeth.
Flirtation finds you
in the middle of a noisy crowd
and sneaks your mind off
to a hidden corner
suggesting outlandish
otherworldly
unlikelihoods
so convincingly
that you wait for them
to happen
never imagining
you had them in you
and you don't
or at least
you might not
but maybe you will
or perhaps you won't.
Hinting at what could be,
flirtation obscures the difference
between Yes and its unreliable cousin, Maybe.
Flirtation resides in the present,
driving No and all her kin
into an exile of the future,
where it might not happen
after all.
Open and endless are the possibilities
that seat themselves in the present
without regard for more.
Encouragements like

120

Could, Might, Maybe, and We'll See.
Although perhaps you won't
or at least you might not,
but maybe you do
or else you don't.
Flirtation tilts its head
proposing the unsuggestible
and touches with a whisper
that you
are worth
the wait.

Collector

She amasses friends
the way children collect coins
and stamps and baseball cards.

Counting them out,
one by one,
trying to complete the set.

She treasures the collection
more passionately than
any single one.

Her lovers accumulate
like dust on her shelves.
The photographs on the wall

map a geography of faces,
posed and unposed,
frozen and framed for display.

Sipping brandy in the quiet winter nights,
she imagines a future that looks like a past
that never took place,

as she browses a scrapbook
she calls memory
and shrouds herself in her collection.

Evenly Matched

Your word against mine
and mine jealous.
The air thickens
as we spit syllables
that collide
and stick
and hang between us
like smog.

Evenly matched,
we inhale accusations
exhaled by each other
and I wonder
what malignancies grow
in laboratory mice
exposed to high levels
of jealousy.

Descent

We met two men
on their upward climb
as we came down the trail.

Each man with heavy wool socks,
neatly trimmed mustache
and tight short shorts.

They smiled at us and asked
if we'd seen bears, then about weather, water, terrain.
My lover said "No one between you and the peak"

My blush melted into laughter
while the four of us passed knowing nods
and they teased about the fact

that our backpacks were bigger
and our legs hairier
than theirs.

We saw them again
at a midtown restaurant.
Our hairy legs played footsy

under the table as we waved.
They asked nervously about
the food, the service

(No one asked about bears),
and then they introduced us
to their wives.

Her Toes

I wanted to love her toes.
They were short and knobbed at the ends.
Top sheet pulled from its tidy tuck,
her toes peeked at me from the far end of the bed.
Laced with black wires, capped with thick cracked nails,
looking across the full length of my nakedness, her toes
        stared at me
as she slept. I wanted to love
her toes the way I loved her thighs, her laughter, her grey
        eyes
as we lay draped by covers fallen in the haphazard that
        follows
an explosion. Sunlight crept between the blind. A shadow
        caressed
her face. I kissed her forehead and stroked her hair. I
        wanted to love
her toes as we lay draped in the haphazard that follows
        eruption.
The city after an earthquake. The foam that trails the blast
of a shaken can of beer. Dust scattered by wind after
        volcanic burst.
Radiation's random fall from mushroom clouds. Bed sheets
        settling upon
two women.

I wanted to love her toes but the only indication of waking
        she gave
was a slight turn at the corner of her mouth. She smiled to
        feel
her own body warming beneath my touch. I loved how she
        rocked,
wordlessly, evenly and easy. When her hands set out
in search of my contours,
she rolled to face me.

Fingers danced across skin, ducked around corners
and leapt for the moon.
When she found what she was looking for
her lids finally lifted.
Two thick yellow toenails grinned at me
from beneath her brow,
and I turned to stone
at her fingertips.

I wanted to love her toes,
but time ran out on us.

Double Edge

You like your razors disposable
Not the old-fashioned ones with bone handle
And exposed blade
But the sleek new ones
With swivel heads.

You like your razors disposable.
Light in your hand
Angled to slide along shins
With subtle strokes of smooth.

You've always enjoyed a close shave.
No rough patches, no nicks, no foamy mess.
Just a quick, shapely, comfortable clean.

When blade goes dull,
Toss it out,
Get a new one at the corner store.

You like your razors disposable.
Cheap, easy to use, cheap.

Pick up a new one if the old one cuts you.

Rejection

They circle around
laughing at me—
the fifth-grade boy who ran away
from my kiss when I spun the bottle at him,
the cousin who didn't want me in the game
then wouldn't pass the ball when I was free in the end zone,
the coach who told me "too short,"
the boyfriend who called me "too fat,"
the boss who promoted everyone but me,
and every woman
in every bar
who ever looked me over
and turned away.

I feel them crowding around
laughing with one another
sipping cocktails
and naming my flaws
but you are the only one here
across the table from me.
You are the only one
turning away now
asking me out of your life
telling me I'm too much of this
and too little of that.
I try to push the others out
to keep my eyes locked on you
but each time you blink
I feel your lids
like a guillotine
on my wrist
and I hear them all
howling with disdain and disgust
as they find fault

even with the way
blood flows
from my
vein.

Wedding Vows

Driving home for the wedding
of my high school bestfriend
I shift to neutral and cut the engine
at the birch tree that marks the spot
I used to coast the Volkswagen down the hill
and silently roll up the driveway.
Today, there's no need to creep
undetected past sleeping parents.

I coast past Kim's driveway
and imagine her fussing with her mother
about the thickness of eyeshadow,
the plunge of her neckline,
the same details they argued every Saturday night.
Kim's mother begged her daughter to dress down,
"not so provocative."
My mother encouraged me to dress up,
"look like a lady."
An unlikely pair of friends,
I, the big-boned soccer goalie
who never wore anything but jeans.
Kim, the big-busted cheerleader
who wore tank tops, mini skirts, and heels.
Inseparable through high school,
we drove to parties together,
but Kim usually found her own rides home.
The next day, she would trust me
with such precise details
of backseats and boyfriends
that I couldn't doubt her words.
"You'll be my maid of honor"
Kim told me while revealing the hickey
hidden by her turtleneck sweater.
"Are you still a virgin?"

she wrote me at college.
Later, she visited me
when I was working in L.A.,
and the same question,
still unanswered,
echoed from the past,
an unspoken wall
between us.

A banker now, Kim deals loans.
More than time stands between us.
She wrote to me about her groom,
a software wiz who drinks beer with a lime.
Twice the age she was
at her Sweet Sixteen party
when we vowed "No secrets,"
Kim walks white down the aisle
with someone I don't know
as maid of honor.
I fail to recognize her kid brother
and her father looks through me when I wave.

In the receiving line, Kim marvels at my hair.
Ruffling her hand through my crewcut,
she tugs the spike in front,
and giggles at the braid in my tail.
When she asks "What's new?"
I find little room for truth,
having promised myself
not to say anything
she doesn't know
how to hear.

My secrets are locked
in the morning moment at home
when my mother struggled to braid my tail.
Wispy strands kept slipping through her fingers.
"Just cut it off for the wedding," Dad called,

"It'll grow back soon enough."
"But Dad, my girlfriend holds it when we dance."
"Well, I wouldn't want you to stop dancing," he called back.
Mom kept braiding,
but I could see in the mirror
that she was behind me smiling.
The smile stayed with me
long after the braid was gone.

Two Approaches to a Single Problem

Can you be more specific?

It's just a knot.

What kind of knot? A slip knot? A half hitch?
Is it a carrick bend or a reef knot?

I dunno, just a knot.

Well, what about the knife?

Yeah, a knife.

What type of knife?
A pocket knife? A hunting knife?

Medium size—it could fit in your hand.

A switch blade? A Bowie knife?
A kitchen knife or carving blade?

I'm not sure. What difference does it make. It hurts!

OK, where does it hurt?

I told you, right here.

Where there? Be precise. Your stomach?
Your liver? Is it your kidneys?
Your heart?

I don't know! Deep!

How deep?

*I told you. When I see you
it feels like you're
sawing through
the knots in
my gut
with a
rusty
blade.*

Losing Patience

There's little left to say for patience.
My father told me if I studied hard,
geometry would come.
It never did.
My brother took me to the lake,
and when he left with two perch and a trout
I remained till nightfall,
patient and fishless.
My mother taught me to wait out boyish men
sowing oats on other girls,
but all that did
was postpone the realization
I wasn't interested in them anyway.
Patience and indifference are not the same.
Now, my lover tells me she needs to see other women:
"If you love me,
you'll be patient with me" she says.

I like to pick my nose when I'm alone.
I rarely come up empty handed.

What I Learned in Girl Scouts

A clove hitch will hold
if you are securing both
ends and the tension remains
constant in opposing directions.
A half-hitch will do when you want
to tie a loose end to a rooted one.
A reef knot will hold two unattached cords together
while a cat's paw anchors with gravity's pull.
A slip knot suffices for temporary connection,
yet a true lover's knot will look much like a slip knot,
but won't slip.
And only an experienced eye
will see that subtle difference
between a true lover's knot
and a noose.

How I Want It

You light your cigarette:
a quick strike,
a long hard draw,
a single blaze.

You light your cigarette,
and smoke drops
from the side of your mouth,
Ashes flicker to the floor.

By the way you light your cigarette
I know what you want,
and by the flick of ash
I know how you want it.

You light your cigarette
and when you offer me the pack
it is easy
to decline.

My Morning Jog

I am melting
in a substitute
for your arms
as sunbeams stroke
each step
of my morning jog.
Lifted across lakes
cleansed by waterfalls
wrapped in rainbowed mist
I swim in the rush
of a liquid luxury
that gives texture
to a memory filled
with moments of you.

Streaming with sweat
from running up mountainsides
I collapse against a tree trunk
in joyful exhaustion
moist soil
barky roots
entwined

I listen
for your heartbeat
amid pine needles and moss.
Renewed by a golden sunrise,
I bend my eyes
to find the hermit thrush
singing the lonely song
of our separation.
I wonder if you
are awake
watching the sun rise

where you are
and if your smile
awaits me
again
in tomorrow's dawn.

The Changing of Seasons

White puffs of air
dissolve in the autumn chill
as my breathing loudly marks time
with my footfall.
Trotting through wooded trail
I chase my youth,
as if one step will launch me back
into the lean legs of the athlete
I used to be.

I let the lake's edge lead me
as I race along at a pace
my dog only walks quickly to.
She follows in my wake
taking leisurely sidetrips
sometimes out of sight
but always within earshot
to drink, cool off,
simply to romp.

I hear her crash through brush
plunge into the lake
and crash back to my side.
Her tongue and tail wag delight
at our reunion.
Wet and kicking mud,
she looks to me for approval.
In return, I offer only the whisper
of strides sifting through fallen leaves.

The sun is slowly disappearing
into the pines
and my dog darts off
in eager pursuit of a squirrel

she won't catch.
I do not break my gait to wait.
I know she will fall in beside me,
panting her own clouds of cold
stepping her own canine strides.

We leap over the dry rut
that will flow a stream in spring.
My breathing quickens.
My step slows.
My dog stops for a moment to sniff.
She senses things I cannot know,
but in the whisper of my stride
I can hear the end of a day
and the changing of seasons.

Resolution in Moving On

perhaps that love we wanted
will be waiting for us
in another
lifetime

but this long, slow healing
has been worth
our coming together, our sharing
and our separation

we cannot return
to where we were
but we have found resolution
in moving on

and although each compromise
carries a cost,
we both collected
beyond our debts
when we forfeited our bond

each touch has reshaped me
each kiss has strengthened me
each moment of loving
and being loved
has made me
new

the loves that await me
have only been made possible
by you
bringing me
to where
I am
now

142

Giving a Daughter Away

Charlie McVay could finish *The Times* Sunday crossword puzzle in a single sitting, but he could never remember where he parked his car at a shopping mall. He was the same way with his family—he could handle a crisis when it came along, but the little things sometimes tripped him up. He was an architectural engineer whose job it was to worry about the structural aspects of building, not the trimming on eaves or the flutes on columns. Charlie McVay made sure the buildings his firm designed would remain standing.

When Charlie's youngest daughter, Eleanor, called him at work to announce that she was getting married, Charlie knew that it would be his job to help his wife get past the fact that their son-in-law was going to be Jewish.

"I know Mom is pretending not to notice that Howard is Jewish, Dad, but I also know that we're talking about marriage now, and Mom is going to have to deal with that," Eleanor said. With an added element of plea in her voice, she added "I thought maybe you could lay a little groundwork before we make the official announcement."

Charlie paused from an apartment complex sketch he was working on. "Howard is a great guy, Eleanor. Your mother and I both like him," Charlie reassured his daughter. He began doodling a cake with a bride and groom perched on top and thought of his wife's lengthy list of Howard's flaws: He's balding (Charlie pencilled a top hat on the groom's head), he laughs like a choking goose, he likes to hunt, he's too quiet, and he's not Catholic.

Unlike her husband, Marie McVay took details very seriously. She would go to a restaurant and comment on the type of silverware, the waiter's lisp, and the ratio of oil to vinegar in

143

the salad dressing. Howard was always amazed by how attentive his wife was, but he never knew what the final count of her observations would yield. By Charlie's standard, Marie had a twisted notion of math. Sometimes the sum of her endless complaining would be a perfect evening. Other times, she would pile compliment upon compliment, only to add it all up to disaster.

Charlie was convinced that his wife would embrace Howard as her son-in-law, if for no other reason than her impatience for grandchildren. Some details, after all, took precedence over others.

"Honey, your mother has spent the past few years rubbing her rosary raw for you girls to get married," Charlie told his daughter. "She's been tending that garden out back ever since you left for college, and I think the idea of planning your wedding is one thrill she's been keeping her nurturing skills tuned for. Besides, she likes Howard—we both do."

"I know you like him, but I want him to feel part of the family. Anyway, I called Mom. Howie and I are having dinner at home this Friday with you and Mom. I just thought I'd give you a little advance notice."

"Your mother is going to be as pleased with this news as I am, Ellie. Congratulations! Have you told Howard's family? Have you chosen any dates or anything?"

"Well, we were hoping that you and Mom could meet Howard's parents soon. We think June is as good a month as any, and it gives us three months to plan. We haven't told anyone yet—except Kate. I called her yesterday and asked her to be maid of honor. She ought to be finished with her dissertation by June."

"Sounds like all systems are 'Go.' How is your big sister these days?"

144

"She said she couldn't wait to meet Howie and asked me to go simple in planning her dress. Typical Kate."

Kate McVay was six years older than Eleanor, and she had been living in the Southwest for almost five years doing archaeological field work and trying to finish up her doctoral thesis. At the mention of her name, Charlie started sketching the elder of his two daughters.

While Eleanor had always been only too eager and able to please her mother, Kate was the one who had often driven Marie McVay to cry "Where did we go wrong?" It was Kate who arrived home late for dinner when she was eight with eleven garter snakes slithering around inside her T-shirt. "I won! I kept all the snakes in my shirt longer than any of the guys could. Look!" and she tugged at her collar to untuck her shirt, unleashing snakes in every direction onto the carpet. Later, in high school, it was Kate who said Confession was just "a priest's way to get his jollies" and then she would not make Confirmation because she said she didn't believe in "all that Pope shit." Kate dropped out of college to "find herself" and called Charlie at work to let him know she was safe—living in a commune of some sort in the Caribbean, letting her hair turn into snarls and listening to lots of reggae music. Charlie convinced himself it was better than her following Jim Jones or becoming a Moonie and decided Marie did not have to hear all the details of their daughter's adventures.

Whenever Charlie sketched Kate, he began with her eyes, then her smile, and a pair of thin tight braids. She hadn't worn braids since she was fourteen—he didn't count the dreadlocks she wore for a few years—but he liked to remember her with long, combed hair.

"How's her research going?" Charlie asked.

"Oh, the same, I guess. We mostly talked about the wedding. You know, girl talk."

145

When Friday arrived, dinner went smoothly. Howard handed Marie a bottle of white wine at the door, and Marie said it would go perfectly with the fish she was preparing. Charlie would not have noticed that Eleanor was wearing the sweater that he had given her for Christmas except that Marie made note of the fact. There was an awkward moment when Howard coughed up a tiny fish bone, but that was the only hitch in the evening. When Marie poured out the Sanka, Eleanor took Howard's hand, took a deep breath, and announced their plans for a June wedding.

Marie wept happy tears, Eleanor joined in, Charlie and Howard looked at one another, shrugged and smiled politely with only a flutter of embarrassment at not knowing what to say and having to wait out the tears.

As soon as the lovestruck couple left, Marie was on the phone with her best friend, Clare.

The next day, Eleanor phoned her father at work to thank him for "helping Mom past the details."

"Ellie, you and Kate don't give your mother enough credit sometimes," Charlie said. "All she wants is to see you two girls happy."

When Charlie hung up, he realized that he had spoken for himself too—all he wants is to see his two girls happy. He is proud of both of his children, he knows that each has her own sense of independence, but he still likes it when they call on him for advice or lean on him for help.

Now Charlie sits in his office mapping out plans for a local shopping mall. The phone rings.

"Can you believe it, Dad? My kid sister is grown up enough to be getting married! I talked with her last week when she was worried that Mom might not like the idea of her becoming a Kaufman, but last night she said it was no big deal."

146

Ellie Kaufman—Charlie hadn't thought about the erasure of his own name from his daughter's identity. Eleanor Kaufman—he is sure it sounds pleasant enough on the ear, but it still grates in his ear with an unsteadiness, a lack of permanence. Charlie assures himself he will adjust.

Charlie loses a bit of the conversation, but falls back into it as Kate says "Howard must be a great guy. Ellie's really excited. She says she wants to wear Mom's wedding gown."

"Yeah, the two of them were digging through the attic this morning looking for it. They called me to ask if I knew where it was. Seems that your ski equipment and camping gear make it pretty hard for anyone to find what they're looking for." As Charlie speaks, he draws dashes to mark parking spaces around the shopping mall.

"Ellie wants me to fly out this weekend to get fitted for my dress. She wants me to be the maid of honor." Charlie hears a hint of reluctance in Kate's voice just as he finishes detailing the parking lot with a few trees and a flag pole.

"Of course she does, Kate. You're her only sister."

"I'm not sure I can, Dad."

"Well, if this weekend is bad, I'm sure the dress can wait. I'll take care of the ticket arrangements as soon as you let me know when you can make the trip for the fitting."

Charlie lifts his drafting pencil from his plans and scribbles "Call travel agent" on a scrap of paper. Then he begins sketching Kate's picture, trying to imagine how she will look at the wedding. He starts with her eyes and her smile, but isn't sure what to do with her hair, so he moves to her body—wide shoulders V-ing down to a slender torso. By the time he completes her legs, he realizes that he has drawn her in slacks.

"It's not just the dress fitting, Dad. I'm not sure I want to be in the wedding. Why doesn't Ellie ask Beth Maloney or Brenda Halpern? What ever happened to her college friend she Eurailed with?"

"Kate, this is your only sister's wedding you're talking about!" says Charlie as he is scribbling short hair with a long streak of bangs falling diagonally across her face, covering one eye.

"It's not that I don't *want* to be there. Well, I do and I don't. It's hard for me, that's all."

"Kate, you're not making any sense. Why on earth would you not want to be in your sister's wedding?"

"I turned thirty-four last week."

"Yeah, and you turned thirty-three a year ago, and you'll turn thirty-five next year. So what? When did you start worrying about your age? C'mon, Kate, what's up?"

"I don't like weddings, you know that. Too formal, everyone 'oohing' and 'ahhing' and crying over public vows as if somehow something changes between the two people."

"Oh, Kate, even you can 'ooh and ahh' a bit for your own sister, can't you?" Charlie looks at his drawing and sees that Kate has never been the ooh-ahh type. When he used to take her to see the Patriots, she's scream "Stick it to 'em, Tony" every time Tony McGee broke through the line.

"I know, Dad, but . . ."

Charlie, who expected any wedding crisis to originate with his wife, does not want to hear any but's from his daughter so he says "Can't you just do this as planned for your mother? Or think of your sister for that matter—wouldn't you want her to help make your wedding perfect?"

148

At first, the long pause over the telephone wires convinces Charlie that he has found the right track to take with his daughter. Then the pause allows him to recall the series of excuses Kate has had in recent years: I know I could go to school nearby, *but* the archaeology programs are better out West; I want to come home for Christmas, *but* I have to get my thesis finished; I'd like to see you soon too, *but* I only have one week between school and this project, so I'm going to Mexico with a friend.

"Dad, you know I never want to screw things up for you, but . . ."

"But what?"

"Well, I've been thinking about the whole idea of marriage and wedding rituals, you know, fancy dresses, high heels, till death do us part, and it seems, well, like it's not my style."

"It's not *your* wedding, Kate." Charlie starts outlining a gown on the figure he has drawn, but he cannot get it to look right.

"I know it's not my wedding, Dad, but . . ."

"So think about Eleanor, will you? After all, this is her wedding."

"Dad, I'm not thinking about Ellie right now, because I'm trying to tell you about me."

"Well, then, what about you?"

"Dad, I live with the woman I love, and that makes it very difficult to come home to celebrate Ellie's wedding while I have to continually lie about my own relationship—that's what."

Charlie knows what he has heard. There is no mistaking "woman," but only half of him hears the word. The half of

149

Charlie that always hoped Kate would find an outdoorsy guy, athletic and articulate, to go hiking with and to ball games—that half of Charlie can't believe what he has heard and asks Kate to repeat it.

The other half, the half that heard right the first time around, wonders if he messed up by teaching his daughter to fly fish and throw a fork ball.

There's a third half that now understands why Kate has been so secretive at times, rarely comes home for holidays. That third half of Charlie realizes that he has not been the only one hurting by Kate's absence and it must have been that half of him controlling the pencil as he drew his daughter in jeans and a sweatshirt.

"Linda and I have been living together for the last four and a half years, Dad. We're in love, too, but nobody has been sending out announcements and inviting us to march down the aisle."

The half of Charlie that knows it all makes sense hears his daughter telling him who she is, but that half can't find any words. The other half sits in an angry silence.

Kate keeps talking, and when she says "I'm telling you all this because I love you." Charlie realizes that neither of his daughters has ever said those words to him before. Then he thinks about Linda, who is no longer just his daughter's roommate. He remembers the one time he visited the two of them. He thought Linda was great—a long ponytail, freckles, and an endearing gap between her two front teeth. He thinks about the ways his daughter is strong and knows how much of himself he sees in her strength.

"I thought that you might have already figured it out, Dad," Kate says, waiting for any response beyond silence.

"How could I have known?" he asks, and his pencil begins drawing a second figure, taller than the first, with a ponytail, freckles and a wide smile with a gap between the two front teeth. Charlie is amazed by how much detail he recalls. The memo says "Call travel agent," and he writes "two tickets" and then draws a big question mark below the words.

"I know the wedding isn't the best time for me to be bringing this up, Dad, but it hurts me to watch Ellie bring her lover into the family while I have to hide mine."

Half of Charlie wants to say "As long as you are happy, I'm happy for you," but the other half speaks. "What the hell do you expect me to tell your mother?"

"Tell her that her daughter is a lesbian."

Silence.

"Tell her that her daughter is a lesbian who has been living with her lover for longer than her other daughter has even known the man she's going to marry. Maybe you could add that this wedding is a perfect time for the family to welcome in all the in-laws."

"I can't tell her that!"

This time it is Kate who remains silent.

"Does Ellie know any of this?" Charlie beings tracing over the question mark, making it darker and thicker.

"No, I thought I'd start with you. I thought you might help get Ellie and Mom used to the idea before Linda and I arrive."

"I don't know what to say," says Charlie because he doesn't.

151

"Well, Linda and I are going camping this weekend. I'll call you on Monday." Kate's voice sounds steady and patient to Charlie.

On Sunday, Charlie struggles with the crossword puzzle. Clues keep pointing him in the wrong direction. It saddens him to write "solo" in response to the clue "To perform alone." He can't come up with a five-letter word for "unconcealed" or the name of King Lear's loyal daughter. The car racing acronym "NASTAR" reminds him of the time he took Kate to a Demolition Derby for her tenth birthday, and too many of the answers require knowledge of pairs: "Sonny's onetime partner" for Cher, "Jungle Twosome" for Tarzan and Jane, "British Duo" for Prince Charles and Lady Di. When "Geriatric hair color" turns out to be "pepper and salt," Charlie has all the pairings he can take and puts the unsolved puzzle down.

Marie, who had been in the backyard moving some potted plants into the garden, comes in for a glass of water. After filling her glass at the tap, Marie sits down on the couch, facing Charlie. "Finished with your puzzle, dear?" It was more of a statement than a question.

"No, there's still quite a bit unanswered," Charlie replies.

"You're not giving up, are you?" Marie has never seen Charlie leave any blanks in a crossword.

"I'm not in the mood. That's all."

"Everything seems different now, doesn't it?"

"What do you mean?" Charlie asks, wondering what has changed for his wife.

"Well, as I was planting, I kept thinking about what it means to be a mother and to finally let my little girl stand on

152

her own. As I patted the dirt around the tiny roots, I realized what a great risk one takes in letting go. I spent the whole morning thinking about Eleanor."

"I spent the morning thinking about Kate." Charlie doesn't know if he wants to pass on Kate's news. He isn't sure which half of him will do most of the talking. He also doesn't like recognizing how varied his feeling can be.

"Kate? Why Kate?"

"She called me at work on Friday."

"She did? Why didn't you tell me? Is everything OK?"

"She phoned to say that she hopes we'll invite her roommate, Linda, to the wedding so that she'll have someone to make the trip with."

"Well, Eleanor didn't say anything about it, but if Kate thinks we should, of course, we'll invite her roommate. What else did she have to say?"

"Oh, just little things—like that she was going camping this weekend. We talked about everyday details and it has me thinking about how easy it is to lose track of the ways children grow up."

"Well, sometimes you've kept a little better track of Kate than I ever could. At times, it's better not to know everything."

"Do you really believe that?"

"Yes and no. I have had to know an awful lot about my family to know what I do and don't want to hear. I've watched you do your crossword puzzles for over thirty years, and I have

153

never understood why you think you're not finished until you have every square filled. I don't need to have every square filled to solve some puzzles."

Charlie couldn't remember his wife ever being so philosophical. He knew that he had kept information from his wife in the past, and he had always felt as though it was against her will. It had never dawned on him that she might be exerting a control of her own in these matters.

Passing on Kate's disclosure to Marie suddenly lost a great deal of importance. If nothing else, Charlie's wife was right about how differently the two of them approached puzzles. Although he didn't know if or when his wife would ever learn the details of Kate's relationship, Charlie knew that his daughter had presented him with a puzzle, and he was going to find every answer.

IV.
Love
Flowers

Thighs I Have Known

Thick and muscular
beneath flapping kilts
they have flexed themselves
up and down field hockey fields

Hugged by tight jeans
worn soft and white with wear
they have waved to the world
through tiny windows of tattered threads

Long and lean
they have winked at me
through narrow slits
of black leather skirts

In their absence
a wheelchair's smooth ride
attends to practical purposes
as biceps steal the limelight

Soft with blonde fur
bleached gold in summer sun
they have slipped between cool sheets
to lock me in embrace

Straddling bicycle seats
poised to steal second base
shaven smooth as glass—
These are the thighs I have known

Their shape
their function
their motion
their strength

Thighs
have it
over calves
by a leg length

Those powerful levers
that have carried lovers
to me
and away

Outgrowing the Fairy Tale

The first time
I ever heard the word
"Dike"
My mother was reading to me
About a little Dutch boy
Who saved his village
By plugging a hole in the
Dike
With his thumb.

Now, I stuff back issues of *Bay Windows*
Into brown paper bags
As if students might peek in my trash
Or some bag lady will start a scandal
By waving my old newspapers on Main Street.
I mark a box "L" for *Lesbian Connection*
Ready to explain it as "Leftist Writings,"
But no one ever asks, and, in bold moments,
I wish they would.

The words I use to name myself
Vary with my mood
But always it's my "friend"
When I mean my "lover."
And there she is adorned in all the clues—
Cropped hair, leather jacket, uneven earrings, and tattoo.
"Does what I look like really matter?" she asks,
And "Why do you care what your neighbors think?"
No answer.

When family and friends make plans to stop by,
I mock my pig-sty tendencies by telling them
They'll have to wait until I straighten up
The apartment. They never know what truth

Keeps them uninvited.
Caught off-guard by drop-in guests,
I fret over whether it's best
to sneak *OUT/LOOK* off the table
Or pray it blends in with *Time.*

I used to substitute
When telling stories—
A "he" for every "she."
Eventually I ceased
Using pronouns altogether,
Except when I was with
Her
And it was time to talk about
Us.

But it grew so dark in the closet
That we had trouble
Telling one another
Apart.
Now, I'm trying to pull myself out
Of those stories I told
As if about someone else.
I'm trying to unearth
The truths about me.

Now, I take time to feel
The rush in my heart
Before checking over my shoulder
To see who saw her touch my arm
Or if anyone sneered when we brushed together.
More and more
I know our actions are right
And the world twisted by its own fear.

Now, I even find myself reaching
To touch her as we walk the streets.
I lean on her as the bus turns a wide corner.

Last week I said "dyke" in a restaurant.
When the guys at the next table
Looked over with obvious displeasure,
I did not pretend
To be talking about
A dam in Holland.

I too have tried to save the city for too long.

Syzygy

Syzygy, syzygy, syzygy—
who wouldn't want
such a buzz of a word?
The hum of it sparks
the same ripple set off
when one tongue slides down
the smooth of my throat
while a second
slips between thighs.
Syzygy whispers
to make a body quake.
It tickles and tingles,
meanders and mingles
with all of the sights
and the sounds of the riddle
that bring both the near
and the far
to the middle.

Wingbeats of angels
sweeping time under stars,
syzygy fashions an explosive mirage
that blasts yesterdays into a single today
born on the evening we spent,
we three,
in what the French call
a *ménage*.

Syzygy,
who wouldn't want
such a buzz of a word
when translations are so hard
to come by?
Syzygy: "the nearly straight-

line configuration of three
celestial bodies
in a gravitational system."
Oh, I need the word now
when the firmament calls.
I am aching with syzygy's pull.

I Was Lucky

My friend assures me
we won't be held up
but they take him away
to the border house
and leave me to answer
for my American passport
issued in Johannesburg.

In their minds
we are the ones
who posed as tourists
and shot up the capital city
killing bystanders and guards in Gabarone.
Gabarone—no bigger than my hometown
in Massachusetts
where I never imagined a man
would touch an AK-47 to my crotch
and I'd believe him when he'd say
that I was lucky.
"I pull the trigger" he says
"and *that* would be bad luck for you."
At the border between
what used to be Rhodesia and Botswana
I hear the news of three attacks
because I am accused of one.

Those stories that thickened the smoke
at shebeens in Soweto flash at me
in the dark green lenses
of my interrogator's aviator eyes:
A bag over her head
Trifosa was raped
for having a brother
who was seen talking to a friend

of a friend
of a suspected ring leader.
Dumi's broken nose
puffed her eyes shut for days
when she could not name
the organizers of the march.
Kulele's back a book of flesh—
the cipher of cross-stitched scars
etched by the whip of a sjambok
braided with rhino hide
and tipped with lead.

At the border
I try to trace
my last month of travel:
Nights beneath the Southern Cross.
Days viewing springbok, kudu, giraffe.
Even I begin to doubt my word
as they place photographs before me
of damage done at a U.N. camp in Lusaka,
at private homes in Harare,
and at a school in Gabarone
where I was two hours before
the hour of attack.

I explain ammo crates
on top of our jeep
to keep lions off our food.
Original passport?
"Stolen—Issued in Boston—Call them!"
His teeth flash in a grin
I cannot identify as kind or curdling
because reason is not to be trusted.
I don't know the names
they ask about,
I've never been to places
they say I've been,

and when they tell me my friend is a spy—
that he's confessed it to them—
I realize all I know
is his favorite beer,
his love of back rubs,
his eye for springbok and kudu.

"It was a jeep just like yours
that opened fire on the school."

In and out of three tiny rooms
four hours without seeing my friend
I cling to my truth as best I can
and they make no apologies
when they reunite us
at the roadside
free to go in the blaze
of a thick red sunset.
We drive six hours
to find a small hotel
and ice for my friend's black eye.
"How's it? You OK?"
"Yeah, how 'bout you?"
A nod and then we hold each other
all night
without speaking
or sleeping.

I Only Walk His Dog

He wears this plague so bravely:
    walking despite sores,
    stepping with confidence to greet me
despite loss of sight,
    talking about the future
    planning with confidence
surprised when the flu knocks him out,
    calling himself lazy
    on days he cannot get up.
"I'm into bondage," he says of the tubes
that tie him to his bed.

He wears this plague so bravely
that when I find the keyhole
I almost see patterns
in the random scratches
etched into the door
by his groping key.

Kinship

I have always
been able to look
Black men in the eye
and see myself,
not all of myself—
not my skin
the color of salmon,
not the thin
straight hair falling on my shoulders,
not my blue eyes or my 34B bra size—
but I have always been able to look
Black men eye to eye.

It was my smile
I saw
mirrored in theirs—
mine, the promise to them
I was not afraid,
not thinking of penis size,
vertical jump, or rhythm;
a version of smile
that assures the male world
I am well-mannered and polite;
a guarantee of my gentle nature
and sense of decorum.

When Black men look me
in the eye
I have seen in their dark eyes,
the very flash that is my smile
that tells all men
I will laugh
at their jokes,
make the coffee,

endure their advances
and bear all innuendo in silence.
I have answered rudeness
with a quiet smile.

I have been trained well,
but instruction did not include
understanding.
The righteous anger
of Black women
who have looked me in the eye
without smiling,
who have taught me to please
without polite laughter,
who have bared the flaws
of my suburban White upbringing,
made possible the realization
that when Black men and I
look eye to eye
our smiles hang
on a dishonest hinge
that governs the lid
of a box more destructive
than Pandora's.
And unless we look
closely,
we won't see
how skin color informs one smile,
and sex instructs the other.

It is time to step out
of our place
in the scheme,
time to unhinge the world
and stand together
as we face the evils
eye to eye.

Community Building

Because the news features "Gays in America"
by interviewing well-dressed men with styled hair,
Because straight women in gay bars
fill a female quota without making a place for me,
Because so few act up against epidemics
of cervical and breast cancer,
Because when hatred labels me
I am called dyke, lesbo, and lezzie bitch,
Because too many of my sisters die young and poor
or live to be old and poor,
And because invisibility is a silence that equals death too,
I don't feel like dancing when you say we should all be gay.

Anger as an Accessory

When I see you wearing yours,
we share a split second to decide:
either look away to safety
or risk the explosion
that meeting of eyes
might spark to mark the truth.

Anger, as flashy as a fedora,
as loud as a bowler,
as shifty as a beret—
some days I wear mine tight,
like a turban,
or thick, like a helmet.

I take it off in public
with a gesture as solemn and invisible
as a pledge in court to tell the whole truth,
or I bear my scalp
with a bow so smug and a smile so wide
I could mock the curtsy out of the Queen.

Yours is packed under a cap,
brim turned to the side
as if your head is screwed on too far
or not far enough;
either way, you tell the world,
"Keep Out."

Or you, peeing outside the convenience store,
with yours pulled close to your skull
under impenetrable weave of wool
you wore at night
to stay warm in 'Nam,
but numb has finally set in.

What emotion blinks under
that plastic flashing Viking cap
worn by the woman who wails
with her portable keyboard,
making every song sound
like Joni Mitchell on sedatives?

I think the slow-stepping
babushka who smiles like an aging angel
keeps hers locked away
in one of her tattered paper bags.
I see nothing of anger leaking out
where her scarf is tied at her chin.

I admire their fashion—all—asking myself:
What do we have in common
except an enemy or two,
a few survival techniques,
and our anger tucked out of sight?
I almost always look away to avoid the blast.

172

I Will Feed Sea Gulls

Tossing my head with witty allusion to Blake,
I impress only myself.
Students longing for a commercial break
Let my words escape out windows
Into springtime air
That marks April the cruelest month to me
But time for frisbee and frolic for them.
The classroom floor collects
The best of my literary analysis,
Syllable upon syllable of wisdom
And dust.

I will feed sea gulls when I am old.
They will engulf me,
Hovering high and low for the best angle.
Catching each morsel I toss in the wind,
They will fight over the precious scraps,
Wrestle with what is there,
Pursue the slices that slide past them
On my first throw.
They will scream sea gull screams for crumbs,
And I will always answer
With my best bread.

I will feed sea gulls when I am old.

Eulogy for a Fallen Friend

I don't know where I was when President Kennedy died,
or what I was doing when Reverend King fell.
Harvey Milk was dead for years before
I heard his name, and I am fully
aware of differences between
an assassin's calculated aim
and a driver's failed attempt
to avoid a darting dog,
but Shakti, I grieve
for you now and
think how alone
you must have
trembled at
highway's
edge.
I
wish
I could
have been warmth
beside your shaking body
as you were for mine when my world was turned
inside out by a woman's love
and then again by her departure.
Shakti, you're the only one I never wore a mask for,
the one who sat with me when I needed stillness
and ran wild with me when I needed to let go
of pain, fear, anger and shame.
When neighbors complained of digging, barking, running free,
I knew it came natural to you to be exuberant,
so I defended you for being yourself
and learned to do the same for myself.
You taught me the injustice of leashes
and expectations that chain one to failure in the eyes of
          others.

174

You licked away salt of sweat, tears and lovemaking
with equal enthusiasm, without judgment,
each sniff of my skin a reminder
that you loved all of me,
telling me to look with my own eyes and do the same.
At night, you chewed holes in the underwear
of the one girlfriend I wanted to stay.
Shakti, I think you won her over before I did,
and she's with me now, and we miss
your efforts to squeeze between us in bed—
those wake up nudges for food, constant pleas for attention.
We miss the tinkling of your tags beside us
as we carry the love you shared through streets
where heroes are believed to be those few extraordinary
        individuals
who charismatically lead masses and then become targets
of those whose lives have never been touched
by the ordinary affection of one who asks only affection in
        return.

Good Housekeeping

Since God's spokesmen have so few words
for women,
I follow recipes for goodness
where I find them
written for me:
mixed in the pages of cookbooks,
printed on boxes of powdered soap,
scrawled on rest room walls,
and screamed in poems never published:
For really tough stains, soak overnight.
Steam until tender, then marinate.
A good man is hard to find,
a hard man good to find,
and still you get
ring around the collar.
Apply generously.
Kubla Khan,
Immanuel Kant.
Mighty Mite.
Sprinkle a dash of paprika
Curry to taste.
I just discovered the taste
of women.
Gentle on your hands.
A little dab will do ya.
ACT-UP and Dykes Unite.
Fold in butter, season with salt,
and knead thoroughly until soft
and playful.
Smells like oceanside magic
Tastes like liquid air
LooksSoundsFeels like cascades
echoing in a misted moonlight.
All natural fibers.

176

Machine wash on gentle.
Spin dry.
Tumbling, still wet
Tumbling, heat rising
Tumbling, finally dry
Machine winds down
Fabric floats
to rest at bottom
of drum

Cycle ends
Tumbled dry again.
Pause before reloading.
I wonder which recipe
God uses
for oatmeal cookies.

Proverb

If I had
a cliche
for every crisis,
I'd be a rich woman.

They Released Mandela

Today they released Mandela
and somewhere in America
straining to see over
her rising and falling chest
a fifteen-year-old girl
who speaks the rhythm of drums
with a click in her voice
wakes at 5 a.m.
to watch
via satellite
as her leader walks
through the prison gates
two hemispheres away.

Last week doctors reset
the angles of the wheelchair
that will someday straighten
her spine.
This morning, she lifts
the one limb
she can lift,
raising a fist
while she sits
in the seat of exile.
She has not forgotten
the sound of blood flowing
the flavor of bullets
the heat of death.
She lost her family in Gabarone.
She was at school during a raid
by South African police
who crossed into Botswana
disguised as tourists

pretending to be
on safari.

Today
they released Mandela
but what they did yesterday
still matters.

A Flicker of Light

☆   ☆   1   ☆   ☆

The moon perched high in the black Vermont sky. Amanda Perry's silver Saab Turbo cut the darkness with little regard for the occasional fog patches that lifted off the fields lining the valley and settled into suspension above the pavement. In the glow of her headlights, Amanda saw a hunched furry profile lumbering from the far side of the road as a raccoon approached the double lines that glowed a familiar yellow trail along the pavement. After years of living in Granville, Amanda still marvelled at how much wildlife New England released from the woods at night. Childhood in Boston had afforded her familiarity only with squirrels, chipmunks and pigeons. Not until her work beside African watering holes where vultures flew circles overhead had Amanda learned to look for the life that waddled and scampered far from the screech and roar of cities.

Amanda had purchased a small A-frame hunting cabin hidden on fifteen acres of Green Mountain hillside following a four-year tour of duty as news correspondent covering South Africa. Without even exploring the job offers that awaited her back in New York, Amanda put aside her career as a political analyst to try freelancing as a nature writer. Four years of tracking and writing about the grassroots anti-Apartheid movements of the South African townships had allowed occasional breathing room between assignments to retreat to the grasslands and wildlife reserves. The gait of giraffe, the playful antics of monkeys, the thunder of a lion's roar had rekindled an excitement Amanda had only distant memory of: the far away wilderness adventures Marlon Perkins brought into the living room of her childhood every Sunday night.

After her father slept the late afternoon away on the couch as Howard Cosell's voice droned the play-by-play of NFL games, Amanda's mother phoned for pizza to feed the family

181

during *The Wonderful World of Disney.* Always, while they waited for delivery, everyone gathered to watch Marlon in his pith helmet and rolled up safari sleeves on Mutual of Omaha's *Wild Kingdom.* When the focus was on reptiles, Mrs. Perry took her ironing to the other room. When her younger sister covered her eyes to escape the fact of an owl clasping a fleeing rabbit or a cheetah downing an antelope in full stride, Amanda covered her own gasp with a cheer, knowing it would make her sister squeal in disgust. "You don't have to laugh, Mandy," her sister would whine, "the background music always lets me know when it's over."

☆   ☆   2   ☆   ☆

Almost upon arrival in South Africa in May of 1984, Amanda had the opportunity to see big game. She was investigating allegations that political opponents of Apartheid who had fled to Botswana were being jailed and executed as accused elephant poachers with neither due process nor tangible evidence for conviction. Amanda quickly saw how easily such dealings could be going on when she arrived at the border region. The rural areas left too much room for practical monitoring of police action. The precise number of African refugees living in exile was impossible to account for, and Amanda met dozens of people who knew of abuses, but refused to talk, fearing for their own lives. Since Botswana lacked any means for dealing with the ivory poaching, South Africa's offer to help was difficult to refuse. Botswana's economic dependence on South Africa left local governments powerless to interfere with Pretoria's forces. It seemed more than plausible to Amanda that Pretoria was accomplishing political control behind a veil of wildlife protection.

Amanda's inquiry yielded little that was verifiable. Pretoria claimed all actions of their armed forces to be issues of national security and, therefore, successfully hid behind the press limitations. Botswanan officials deferred to Pretoria with tied tongues. Despite State of Emergency restrictions, Amanda did get a taste of the splendor of those Wild Kingdom creatures. With the aid of a local guide named Tsepho, Amanda scoured the land

182

reserves in a four-wheel drive jeep tracking African game. The thrill of spotting giraffe off in the distance was exceeded only by driving next to them, 30 miles an hour, as they galloped, full stride beside the jeep. Ostrich, zebra, wart hogs—Amanda became familiar with them all. She marvelled at what sort of disbelieving reception early European explorers must have received with their tales of black-and-white striped mules or spotted, long-necked goats. She learned to distinguish the thin, bearded body of the wildebeest from the wide body of the water buffalo. She looked for the shoulder stripe that marked the springbok, the twisting horns of the impala, the bull's eye rump that identifies the water buck and the high curved antlers that gave away the sable.

Elephants could hold Amanda's attention for hours. As she watched thick trunks deftly curling branches up and into their tiny triangular pink mouths, Amanda thought of a schoolboy tucking a heavy stack of books under his arm. She wondered how those first settlers explained elephants to a country of people who knew only sheep and cattle, hedgehogs and cats. The destruction these animals left in their wake was seen in the woodland, salted with uprooted trees and peppered with large dung deposits. Amanda understood why locals were often unconcerned by the dwindling of the elephant population. With poverty what it was in these rural areas, financial rewards, fueled by Western demands for ivory, certainly made poaching a lucrative practice.

Amanda's disgust and sorrow in witnessing the trail of death left by human intruders were far outweighed by her exhilaration at watching animals live out their lives. She delighted in the graceful, sluggish movements of a feeding herd. She was awed by the strength with which they could rearrange the landscape. And she discovered an elephant quickness that she could have never expected the first time a bull elephant turned on her in a mock charge that left Amanda's heart beating as if it would blow a hole in her chest.

The sounds of early evening enchanted Amanda. She wanted to match each noise of the night with the sights of the day.

183

Growls, roars, screeches, chatter, hoots, screams, cries, thumps and thuds combined in a symphony of mystery, and Tsepho did his best to keep up with Amanda's exhaustive "what was that?" reaction to every chuckle or groan from the African air.

☆   ☆   3   ☆   ☆

The leap of Amanda's dog coincided with the startling whir of a family of fat brown and black birds flushing themselves from the Vermont underbrush. A quick squawk was muffled into silence by the flick of Inkomo's head and the young bird fell limp to the ground as the dog tore off in vain after the rest of the flock which had already safely taken to air.

"No, Inkomo! No!" Amanda shouted.

Eventually, the young Rhodesian Ridgeback whose name meant "beast" in Zulu—well, more like "cow"—romped back to his master. "No!" Amanda pointed to the dead bird. Inkomo panted, a small black feather pasted with saliva to the pink tongue bobbing over the side of his jaw. Amanda took Inkomo by the collar, shoving the dog's snout to the bird. "No!" she shouted one more time. "Bad!"

Inkomo cowered a bit, but more from the way he was being held than from any moral regret, Amanda figured. She released the dog, realizing it had only acted on instinct. Although dogs were disruptive partners for nature walks and birding, Amanda enjoyed Inkomo's companionship for over a year in Africa, and she decided a live souvenir was better than the dead ones usually taken from that continent. Amanda was familiar with Inkomo's eagerness to explore ahead and stir up the underbrush. She respected the dog's speed and strength, the attributes that had led colonists to use Ridgebacks for helping to bring down lions.

But Amanda had not trained her dog as a hunter, and she had not anticipated that Inkomo would ever catch any of the birds.

184

The bird looked to Amanda like a pheasant, but smaller and lacking a long pin-tail or iridescent head. A partridge, she guessed. She looked up "partridge" in the field guide to North American birds and found their range limited to Canada and regions west of Ohio. A note in the map margin read: "Introduced unsuccessfully in several other Northwest states." Amanda turned the pages looking for matching marks. She turned the bird gently with her toe for a more complete picture. The entrails had spilled out of the bird from a small wound on its underbelly. Pale green and pink intestines shone with glossy reflections of light. The field guide proved useless.

Amanda satisfied her need to identify the bird by deciding it matched the book's sketch of a young Ruffed Grouse. Her attention was pulled from the dead bird by a clear, crisp "Klee, klee, klee" slicing the silence of the mid-day August sky. Taking Inkomo by the collar, Amanda slowly eased herself toward the call. After locating the profile of a perched bird high in the branches of a dead oak, Amanda zeroed her binoculars in on the hook-beaked face, studying the tear-shaped color pattern which made the bird look like it wept black tears down a white frown.

Amanda thumbed rapidly through the field guide and found the bird—American Kestrel or Sparrow Hawk. It was a swallow-like falcon, "size of a jay." She returned to her magnified view just as the kestrel took to flight. Grey wings beat thickly as the red-backed bird hovered for a while and then dove, plunging into an open field where the grass was too high for Amanda to witness the encounter between bird and prey. Seconds later, the bird rose, empty-clawed, and flew off, Amanda assumed, still hungry.

☆   ☆   4   ☆   ☆

One afternoon while photographing an elephant herd, Amanda almost dropped her camera at the sound of a howl-turned-scream-turned-thud. The clamor was followed by some growling and scrambling, and to Amanda's untrained ear, the sounds passed

185

so quickly into silence that the best she could do was to watch the reactions around her. The baboons who were scampering froze momentarily, but went back to their business far more easily than Amanda could. None of the elephants appeared to notice the scrape. Amanda headed back to the jeep to ask Tsepho.

"A kill," Tsepho announced.

"What kind? How far from here?" Amanda fired questions.

"Lions probably got a buffalo, maybe a wildebeest. Not far from here, I think."

"Is it safe to look?" Amanda asked.

"Sure, you want to see it?"

"Let's go." Amanda tossed her tripod and camera bag into the back of the jeep, and they were off to a front row seat of the pride's dinner. First the male ate, although the females had done all the hunting. The maned patriarch stuffed himself on and off for about two hours till he looked pregnant, then rolled to the ground to sleep off the gorge. Amanda photographed every detail as long as the afternoon light held out—the tearing of hide, the long tongue lapping up blood and gnawing on choice scraps of meat. The four lionesses seemed to be collaborating on a sculpture as they pared away excess flesh to give shape to a bare-boned skeleton. The two cubs playfully rolled around, dining at their leisure, wrestling one another, and tumbling about the corpse. The sun was setting low behind the Baobab trees before the females and cubs retired from the carcass.

Tsepho and Amanda sat atop the jeep forty feet away and watched. Amanda stayed awake through the night as Tsepho slept wrapped in a blanket on the roof of the jeep. A pair of spotted hyena moved in for a nibble, and Amanda shivered at the heavy pounding of their footsteps, like the gallop of horses, she thought.

186

By morning, the carrion birds were picking at the bones, and a couple of baboons hustled about trying to steal a bite or two. It certainly contrasted the waste that poachers left behind after plucking an elephant of its ivory—like beached whales dragged into a desert, left bloody and dead for the sake of someone's necklace.

☆   ☆   5   ☆   ☆

"Fifteen rolls of a buffalo being devoured? Perry, I sent you up there to investigate the *human* atrocities, and I get back pictures for *National Geographic!*"

"I know, Jim. I know. But I couldn't get an official word out of anybody. Nobody would let me photograph. You know how tightly the police guard their secrets. None of the locals would talk."

"What about this Tsepho character? Couldn't he at least give you the lowdown, a few names?"

Amanda had trouble explaining the poaching situation to her boss, and her loyalty to Tsepho left her no recourse but a simple "I'll do better next time." Amanda took the reprimand as a basic reminder that politics was what South African news coverage was all about.

"How about a story on the workers' compounds, Jim?" Amanda suggested.

"You have any leads? You'll need a contact, you know."

Tsepho had given Amanda the name of his brother who was working in one of the mines, living in a compound in Soweto, and trying to organize a union group. "Yeah, sure I have a contact." Amanda was partly trying to save face. She wanted to prove that she could get down and dirty, work the underground.

187

"Check it out then, but stick to the story, will ya."

Amanda smiled, but her boss kept a seriousness that seemed designed to show how important her duties were.

Amanda headed for the township.

☆   ☆   6   ☆   ☆

"Which compound?" the boy selling apples asked.

"How many are there?" Amanda's Volkswagen bug had sailed into Soweto without a roadblock. The city map she purchased in downtown Jo'burg was deceptive in its aerial view of the sprawling township, but fortunately, the few paved roads were well marked. When she realized that what the map called a park looked like a garbage dump, Amanda decided that asking directions might prove useful.

"You American?" the boy asked looking a bit suspicious.

Amanda eyed the knobby-kneed kid, his khaki shorts too tight and the matching short-sleeve shirt that completed his school uniform too big. Another boy sat nearby tending a few ears of corn over coals. She guessed they were twelve and fourteen and guessed neither had been to school recently.

"A reporter?" the boy persisted.

"Why do you want to know?"

Surprised by how guarded the boys seemed, Amanda tried being more friendly. "Hey, how old are you anyway?"

The two boys spoke to one another in their own language, pointed to Amanda a few times, and finally, the younger of the two, the one selling apples, hopped on a rusted bike and rode off down the street.

That was all it took for Amanda to hook up with "the movement." The Comrades, an umbrella name for all the teenagers politically active in "the struggle," were always looking for foreign contacts to get their stories out of the country. The underground network was elaborately non-hierarchical, so on each visit, it was likely that Amanda would have to trust someone new. No one wanted to be seen having repeated interaction with a foreigner. It was usually the Comrades who called the shots for Amanda. They told her when to be where. They told her what to photograph and what to record. No names. No faces in photos. Amanda realized very quickly that trust, on both sides, was essential. Since they were all breaking the State of Emergency Laws, if the Comrades put Amanda in danger, they put themselves in an even greater danger since the law would look much more kindly on her. They gave her tours of the compounds, arranged interviews with laborers, took her to the illegal drink houses known as shebeens, accompanied her at funerals, so that she would be safe in the sorrow-filled, sometimes hostile, all-black crowds.

The Comrades had access to strike locations and meeting times. Every article Amanda wired out of the country under a variety of pseudonyms owed an enormous debt to the young people who gave her access to the underworld of their movement. Nearly three years after her first venture into Soweto, the trust between Amanda and her compatriots was tested when they brought her to a trial they held for three students who had allegedly informed the police of the Comrades' involvement in an automobile theft.

 ☆　☆　7　☆　☆

After two summer months exploring the dirt roads and hiking trails of central Vermont, Amanda had a solid command

189

of the local birdlife, but she hadn't written a word. She knew how to track the "klee-up" of an Evening Grosbeak to a sturdy yellow-bodied, black-and-white winged bird with a yellow racing stripe along its head. Amanda had a few favorite locations where she could spy on Screech Owls and listen for the mournful whinny that descended into a tremulous wail. With her field guide in hand, Amanda could give a name to every bird that she saw. She kept a list of the birds she saw, but beyond that she had little use for the pad and pen she carried in her knapsack.

Autumn ushered in the Vermont hunting season. Amanda disliked the hunters for glorifying slaughter. They took from the land, for their sadistic satisfaction, the pleasure of con-quering, destroying. "Taking" game, they called it. Amanda heard them talk in the bars of "my deer" or "my bear" even before the season opened, as if in the act of buying a license put a tag on each animal reading "you are entitled to kill me." Although Amanda had never thought of poaching as an American problem, she soon learned from the local warden that hunters were often caught over their "take" limit or hunting out of season. When Amanda grew excited about spotting a Gray Partridge out of its mid-western range, the warden told her that the region had been stocked with Chukar Partridge, according to her field guide, a bird that had been "introduced unsuccessfully in several North-east states."

☆ ☆ 8 ☆ ☆

On a warm December summer morning, Amanda took a phone call at work telling her to meet Sipho as soon as possible at the patients' parking lot of Baragwanath Hospital. The voice on the phone sounded unfamiliar, but the speaker zeroed in on all the right code words. The sky was overcast when Amanda had left Jo'burg for the township, making the air that hung over Soweto seem even greyer than the usual cloud of incinerator ash that sits over the endless rows of matchbox shacks called houses. From her car, Amanda watched the people cut across the large, sandy debris-littered lot across

190

from the hospital. The lot always reminded Amanda of the tourist map she had purchased to navigate the township—the dumping area was marked "Recreational Park" on the map. Amanda had been waiting for no more than five minutes when Sipho appeared at her window.

"Sakubona thisha" Sipho greeted Amanda in Zulu and reached his hand into the open window. They locked thumbs for handshake, fingers wrapping in a shared fist.

"Yebo, sawubona mfana," Amanda smiled as she used the little bit of Zulu her young friends had taught her.

Sipho was a tall and muscular seventeen-year-old with a wide smile, high cocoa-colored cheekbones, small ears, and a head of closely cropped curls. Amanda had met Sipho three years earlier when she was writing a feature on military presence in the high schools. Sipho, as an eager fourteen-year-old, had been beaten by soldiers in the schoolyard when the army had claimed itself necessary to the restoration of order to the school. The soldiers occupied the school as monitors and teacher aids, and prohibited students from gathering in groups of three or more on school property or during school hours. During recess, Sipho had organized a soccer game, and two young Afrikaner soldiers had whipped him with a lead-tipped sjambok and detained him for two weeks without charge. Sipho never returned to school after his arrest.

"What's up, Sipho?" Amanda inquired.

"You must go see if the police are guarding the Emergency Room," Sipho explained. "There was a shooting this morning near Orlando High School. In addition to bullets, the police sprayed tear gas and purple paint so that they can trace down those who were at the shooting. They will wait at the hospitals for people with bullet wounds. No one can go for treatment safely."

191

Amanda got out of the car, looking for purple paint on her young friend's clothing. "Were you at the shooting?"

"No," Sipho replied, "but I'll wait out here just the same. If the soldiers or policemen are in there, we'll need your car to take Khaya to Hillbrow Hospital in the city."

"Has she been shot?" Amanda asked.

"With birdshot," Sipho nodded his head. "We dug most of it out of her legs, but she also got hit in the head with a tear gas cannister. We can't stop the bleeding from her forehead."

Hustling into the hospital, Amanda thought back to her first interview with Sipho. It was shortly after his release from detention, and the interview had resulted in one of Amanda's best articles. Sipho's idealism and hope for South Africa had been woven through her explanation of his experience. Amanda's story had captured the details of detention as well as the spirit of a boy able to see the absurdity of his arrest while also recognizing the importance of not being broken by that absurdity. A year after that arrest, Sipho was whisked off to jail again during a funeral for two Comrades who died in a shebeen raid. Sipho had endured a broken nose during the arrest and multiple whippings during interrogation. When Amanda demanded Sipho's release at the police station, the officer on duty only let Amanda speak with Sipho through a door for five minutes. Later, when Sipho had been released, Amanda asked him if he had been afraid of dying in jail.

"I have always been prepared to die for the struggle," said Sipho, "but now I now I am prepared to kill for it."

Amanda had been inside the hospital a few times before, so she was not surprised when a woman held her baby to her pleading "Udokotela, Ngicel' umsize"—Doctor, please help him. Amanda spotted two policemen smoking cigarettes in chairs behind the reception desk and she had seen enough.

192

Sipho directed Amanda through the township to a house that looked like all the others. He slowly escorted a young girl holding a bandana to her forehead to the car. After quick, quiet introductions, Khaya stretched herself across the floor of the backseat, and Sipho covered her with a blanket. "If we hit a roadblock, tell them you picked me up at the train station because you need me to tend your lawn," said Sipho as he eased himself into the passenger seat.

Amanda followed Sipho's directions out of the township, and rather than risk too many questions at Hillbrow Hospital, she took Khaya to a British doctor she knew in Johannesburg. Amanda insisted that the two rebels spend the night in her apartment in the city and took them back to Soweto the following morning.

Amanda spent the entire day in the township trying to piece together a story about the ways in which the Comrades tended to the injuries of their peers. With Sipho serving as translator and guide, Amanda interviewed a dozen wounded children. They confirmed that one boy had been killed in the shooting, and another, who had reportedly been arrested, could not be located at the police station.

In the late afternoon they returned to Baragwanath Hospital to try to locate the missing child. The nurse at the reception desk told Sipho that the police had been on guard all morning, and no shooting victims had tried to check in.

Darkness was settling over the township as they walked out to Amanda's car. "Can I give you a lift home?" Amanda asked.

Sipho nodded yes and climbed into the car.

"You know where to reach me if you hear anything new," Amanda said as she started the engine. "I'm going to try talking to some of the doctors at Hillbrow tomorrow."

193

"If you need help making contacts, leave a message with Jabu at the taxi stand by the train station," Sipho suggested. "He usually knows how to get hold of me."

Amanda backed her car and headed for the parking lot exit.

"WeAmanda! ake uthula wemoto!" Sipho's voice filled the small interior. "Stop the car!" he repeated in English.

Amanda did, and Sipho leapt out of the car. He ran to a bright red BMW parked amid a row of cars in the staff parking lot and bent down to read the license plate. On returning to Amanda, Sipho was frenzied, unable to keep his feet still, impatient for Amanda to roll down her window. "That car" he pointed. "549 AJP"—Sipho sang the plate numbers again "549 AJP!"

"What about it, Sipho?"

"I saw that car. Two weeks ago. I knew I'd never forget that number: 549 AJP. Follow me. No, meet me at the cemetery across from the power plant. Wait for me there. Do you know where I mean?"

"Yeah, I know it, Sipho. But what are you going to do?" It was unlike Sipho not to answer Amanda's questions, but Amanda took that as even more reason to trust her young guide. So she drove off in the direction of the electrical plant. When Sipho did not arrive after two hours, Amanda grew concerned. She checked her watch often. At 8:00 she decided she would give Sipho until 9:00 and then head back to the city before the curfew would be enforced.

In between the sleep of exhaustion and the consciousness of fear, Amanda heard a blast in the darkness. She looked around and saw nothing. Her watch showed that she had slept, and it was just after 10:00. She turned the key and hoped she wouldn't meet any road blocks on her way out of the township.

194

A thud on her back window would have sent Amanda's knees to her forehead if the steering wheel hadn't stopped them midway to assuming the fetal position. With her foot off the clutch, the car stalled out and Sipho's face was at Amanda's window before she could gather herself enough to sort out her panic. "What the he—" Amanda grunted instinctively.

Sipho ran around the front of the car and hopped in, panting heavily. "Let's get outta here!" he shouted. Amanda's response was a patch of burnt rubber onto the main road.

"The asshole's a doctor! Lives in Randburg—rich suburb—a goddam doctor! I read all his registration papers." Sipho rolled down his window, leaned his head out and remained silent for a while. As they turned back toward the hospital, he pointed to a red and yellow blaze out in the dark lowlands behind the power plant. "There it is—549 AJP," Sipho sighed.

"I worried you'd been picked up by the police. It's after curfew, you know." Amanda knew that Sipho wasn't listening.

"That car tore a boy in two. I saw it. On a Sunday afternoon, kids building toy cars out of coat hangers by the side of the road. Narrow dirt roads, hardly ever any traffic. No one who lives there owns a car. I saw the car and thought it was too fast for the township. I knew it had to be a white man driving. You can't drive like that here. How much of a hurry can you be in? The kid barely looked up. He was four years old. His father's a friend of mine. He pumps petrol in Jo'burg. I watched his son's eyes widen. His mouth open wide in a silent scream. Just a thud— his body flew to the side of the road, his leg remained in the road beside his little wire toy. How could the man not stop? Not even try? He just kept driving as the dirt settled on the dead child and his playmates."

Sipho's voice held no anger. His eyes filled with tears. Amanda could see in the rearview mirror only a flicker of light burning behind them.

195

☆　☆　9　☆　☆

The winter in Granville was more of a struggle for Amanda than hunting season. The snow was deep. The bird population had dropped considerably, and the thick blanket of snow made her outdoor excursions more difficult. Inkomo often grew restless in the cabin, and Amanda wondered if she should have flown south with her birds. Winged visitors to the feeders she hung outside her windows offered minimum solace. Amanda especially liked to watch the Nuthatches swinging themselves up-sidedown on the bird feeder or climbing down tree trunks, head-first, a feat of which few birds are capable. But even these small delights did little to brighten the cold, grey winter.

Amanda felt she had nowhere to go. Ski areas held claim to every inch of mountain that was clear of hunters. Although skiing itself seemed a benign way to enjoy the outdoors, too many of the skiers seemed to stride around the local grocery store as if everyone in Vermont ought to thank them for bringing themselves and their money within the state borders—less violent show of man's ability to dominate than hunting, Amanda thought.

What she hated most, however, was everything she wrote. Her words couldn't capture the exhilaration she felt with life's simple pleasures. She was used to writing of life and death. She knew how to weave the threads of human suffering into a fabric of hope. She had written of teenagers who had built a movement that they were willing to die for, willing to kill for, and she believed that her writing might help them in their struggle for a better life.

☆　☆　10　☆　☆

Sipho met Amanda near the train station. "You can park your car here and no one will notice it," said Sipho. "We'll take a kombi once the others get here."

196

Within fifteen minutes Amanda and Sipho were joined by three more youths—two boys and a girl, all around sixteen or seventeen, Amanda guessed. The girl wore a maroon beret and her school uniform. The boys were dressed in jeans and T-shirts. Together, they hopped a ride in a kombi, a minibus that illegally ran as a township bus. Amanda took in some odd looks from the other passengers, but when Sipho muttered something in Zulu, everyone relaxed a bit, and the driver turned around and smiled: "I never drove for an American newspaper lady before."

The kombi dropped them all in Diepkloof, one of the most impoverished sections of Soweto. The roads were uneven paths of packed dirt between houses. Occasionally, Amanda had found herself driving down dead ends in this sector of town; the map, of course, was useless here. None of the young rebels spoke, and when they walked through a gate and up the path to one of the small brick houses that looked like all the others, Amanda followed. Inside about thirty Comrades had gathered to fill a single room. A large ANC flag of red, green and black draped one wall, and every inch of the other three walls was hidden behind old car tires. The room smelled of rubber and sweat. The dirt floor was lined with tires as seats. Some kids were stacking tires in the back rows, some reclined in them on the floor, and others stood them upright and straddled them as seats. A makeshift table had been set up with a piece of plywood on piled bricks, but all of Amanda's focus remained on the tires.

Throughout the proceedings Amanda tried to note everyone's role in the events. She listened and watched in ways that would give shape to the story she would write. She wanted to reflect the complexity of the trial without passing judgment. She wanted only to report, but her head was spinning with Zulu shouts she could not understand, flesh wounds displayed as evidence of torture, talk of people and places Amanda did not know, name-calling, finger-pointing, and tires everywhere.

Of the three boys on trial, two were brothers who had another brother in the crowd. He had stood up and verified the accusations against the three. No, they did not appear harmed when they returned from their interrogation. Yes, he had heard them badmouthing certain Comrades who were later picked up and jailed. The third defendant had admitted that he knew who had stolen his father's car. Yes, he knew why they had stolen it. "Borrowed it!" someone shouted from the sweating crowd.

Another shout explained "We needed to take a wounded Comrade to a hospital outside the township because the police were standing guard at Baragwanath." The young boy speaking stood and walked to the front of the room as he continued with his story. "Kulele flagged the first car he saw. It happened to be your father, and your father turned his back on the struggle. He threatened to turn us in. Kulele pulled him out and left him unharmed in the road. Mondu died in the backseat anyway. But now Kulele is in jail."

More shouting.

"Amanda, we must all vote the verdict. Is there any evidence that remains unclear? Any questions you would like to ask the defendants?" Kholeka's voice was thickly accented with the click of an upbringing in the Transkei. She was a poised young woman of eighteen with a large face with two round cheeks to match the round breasts that bore Nelson Mandela's portrait on her T-shirt. She had a chip in her front tooth and an open-mouthed smile, but today there would be few smiles. Her words had ushered all the confusion of the day into a new dimension for Amanda.

The testimonies had piled up—interruptions, shouts from the crowd, denials, accusations, anger, fear. Amanda could connect only so much, but she knew what the Comrades were asking when they included her in the jury. She was either with the struggle or she wasn't. She stared at the cannister of gasoline held tightly in the lap of a small boy who had only one arm. "No. I have no questions," Amanda said flatly as if to deny the multitude that were spinning a web in her brain.

"Any summary words from the defendants?" Kholeka asked of the three boys standing, one fidgeting his hands in and out of the pockets, one staring stoically at no one specific, and one offering a final plea. "You all say you are fighting for freedom and justice. Is this what you call justice? Do we stand any chance of being judged fairly?" The boy rubbed the sweat off his high brown forehead and his black eyes narrowed at Amanda, the only white-skinned presence in the room. "The whites are our enemies. Why are we destroying ourselves?"

☆   ☆   11   ☆   ☆

On cold winter nights, Amanda slept on the floor by the wood stove. Occasionally, she would wake Inkomo, sleeping curled at the foot of the sleeping bag, with screams. The crackle of the fire, the flicker of light and shadows on the walls soothed Amanda back into the present.

One late February morning, Amanda and Inkomo awoke to a loud thud. The sun was bright on the snow and when Amanda went to the window to investigate the noise, she saw a small Cedar Waxwing in the snow beneath her. Amanda tugged herself into thermal underwear and stepped into her boots by the door. Inkomo followed as Amanda squeaked across the frozen surface of the snow. Inkomo sniffed the Waxwing, but backed off at Amanda's command. Steam rose gently from the bird as Amanda bent and scooped up the warm, limp body. She stroked the point of the crest before realizing that the feathery chest was rising and falling rapidly. Running her index finger along the belly of the bird, Amanda watched closely, hoping the eyes might open.

"Migration might make your life easier," Amanda whispered to the bird. Between the warmth of Amanda's palm and the whisper in her breath, the stunned bird shook its unconsciousness off. Amanda stood silently cheering as the revived bird flew out of her grasp. Amanda knew she would outlast the winter.

☆ ☆ 12 ☆ ☆

It was dark in the township when Amanda and Sipho were dropped off two miles from the train station. They walked heavily along the roadside, occasionally blinded by oncoming headlights. Every light reminded Amanda of the flames, and she knew today was a story that she could never wire to the States. She had seen the odds stacked so firmly against Sipho and her friends. She too, had risked her own life to tell their story. She never thought it would become her own story quite so fully. And now that it was hers, she knew she could not write it—not until she could distance herself from it.

The necklacing was worse than she had imagined— how could one imagine the smell of burning gas, burning flesh, screaming, crackling, the light of the flames glossing everyone who stood, believing they acted in the name of the struggle? Amanda had endured that light, her vote cast. How could she not? If she was willing to give her own life, those who would take her life could not expect mercy. She had wanted not to look as the tires were fitted over the boys' heads. She only listened to the sloshing of gasoline in the tires, on their bodies. Many had chosen not to watch, but Sipho had insisted they stay. Amanda knew she would have remained even if Sipho had not. She had to live up to her stance. The woof of gasoline igniting. Screams. She too had cast a vote.

Sipho finally broke the silence as they approached the hospital. "I have seen too many of my people killed."

Who still alive is not guilty? Amanda wondered to herself. What consolation was to be had?

☆ ☆ 13 ☆ ☆

Spring in Vermont brought life in every possible shade of green. Deep, dark pine tree green. Pale, yellow grassy green. Soft, white leafy green. Cool, black lake green. Hazy, blue

200

mountain green. So many shapes and shadows of green invited Amanda to indulge in color photography, and she built herself a darkroom in her cabin. She loved the sensation of watching colors and forms appear in the darkness from nothing. She marvelled at the way something as intangible and weightless as light could produce such concrete and graphic images.

Amanda and Inkomo peacefully marched along woodland trails, guiding one another to new places, and living in the present. The local paper had allotted Amanda a weekly column titled "All Creatures," and *Yankee* magazine accepted a story about her effort to trail a flock of Broad-winged Hawks on their migration north. She had submitted a few photographs for publication and started speaking to science classes at schools across the state.

She was billed to students as a naturalist, but inquisitive students often pushed and pulled in ways that tapped into many of her fundamental values. She wondered if it was right to reveal her political opinions to teenagers.

As Amanda's silver car cut through the darkness, she replayed the day's discussion. Although the students enjoyed her photographs, one asked Amanda why, if she could get close enough to get a camera shot, didn't she ever go hunting.

"I don't really like hunting," she had replied.

Another student took to defending hunting, and when the teacher added his editorial, Amanda couldn't help icing the cake.

"Hunting keeps the deer population in check, Miss Perry, so they don't have to die miserably, from starvation."

Amanda wondered if her own retort had been out of line: "Well then—I suppose you could say the same about the

201

role of war in our own species' survival, Mr. Bostock." Amanda wondered if any of the seventh and eighth graders assembled in the school cafeteria understood the comparison.

Inkomo, perched in the passenger seat, seemed entranced by the tiny white reflectors flashing off the guard rails on both sides of the road. The glow of Amanda's headlights showed the profile of a raccoon stepping across the yellow lines into Amanda's lane. Inkomo instinctively stood for a better look, but the swerve of the car pitched him to the floor. With the scream of the brakes, Amanda braced herself on the steering wheel, and locked eyes with the two sparks that marked the animal's frozen stance. She managed to drive clear of the animal and the guard rails, and looked back. The rearview mirror showed nothing but darkness. The smell of the burnt rubber seemed to follow her, and all Amanda could do was drive on.

V.
The
Goddess
Smiles

Disregarding Clocks

Mature according to levels of laughter.
Count embraces, not years.
Measure love.

Counting the Birds in Your Hand

First try the Dewey Decimal System.

Then count the wings
And divide by two.

Or listen at sunrise for the cock's crow.
Once you wake, you will know how many.

Invent your own numbers.
Scramble meanings of words.
Separate the chicks from the cocks

Then subtract the cocks,
Let the hens lay eggs, and multiply by the chicks.
Better yet, let them count themselves.

If you decide to count the feathers before they hatch,
You won't know how many chickens you have,
But you'll discover flight of mind,
And isn't that what feathers are for?

Don't be distracted by the shells—
Brown and white only make for the blessing of variety.
Differentiation is a lie. Some call it an old wives' tale,
But whoever distrusts old wives can be distracted by counting
Sheep.

Why count chickens at all?
Surely, counting is a measure of property,
A sign of ownership,
An account of wealth—
All of which inhibit
Love.

206

Taking Flight

He fashions wings
like Icarus,
to fly past the sadness,
beyond the pain.
Holding his lover's hand
between his own pressed palms,
he is the closest to prayer he's ever been.
Breathing is more labored than dreaming now,
and the face in the mirror peels off
as his bones go liquid inside
and his tears freeze and heal like tiny crystals.
He flies from public outcry
and governmental indifference
to find strength in the fashioning of wings—
feathers of satin, tipped with leather
and made with the weightless bones
of past lovers whose names are already
stitched in the quilt that waits for him.

He fashions wings
not for angels woven with guilt,
but with the fabric of motorcycles and men.
Harley-Davidson, black and chrome,
threaded with chain, lace, velvet and metal.
Then, he embraces the self his family shuns
and when his final breath
sinks into his lover's arms,
it is no surprise that his spirit flies
far past the moon, beyond the sun,
and his body glows with the halo of each star.
Sainted forever,
he is guilty only of loving.

How To Be a Militant Woman

Read the newspaper often.
Preach peace.
Drive an import.
Cover it with colorful bumper stickers.
Speak your mind.
Show your righteous anger.
Point out inequities.
Shave your armpits
but not your legs.
(Hairy armpits make you
a militant lesbian.)
Protest double standards.
Say the f-word often:
Feminism.
Take back the night.
Carry candles when you march.
See connections between
racism, classism, and sexism.
Have a sense of humor
that doesn't target women.
Encourage men to take you seriously.
Care about women's lives.
Demand the knowledge
and right
to control your own body.
Expect others to care
about women's lives.
Pray to the goddess.
Give up red meat.
Don't laugh when it's not funny.
Sit without crossing your legs.
Stand up and be counted.

No Justice

This is not the heaven I hoped for,
not what I expected in the least.
Where are those nifty inventions?
Where are the chains
that bound Prometheus to granite
while eagles feasted on flesh
to remind those who might dare
that stealing fire
has consequences?

Where are all the tidy tasks
customized to each human frailty
and designed to last eternally?
Where are the taloned birds
endlessly tearing the entrails
of those who stole sparks
from atoms
to make
bombs?

Where are the guardians
to set the world right
when mortals trespass
in the realm of the gods?
Where are the hounds chewing
through to the bone
of those who padded themselves
with profits made of skins
darker and deeper than their own?

Why aren't there armies
of leeches
sucking marrow
from those whose commands

set cities aflame?
This is not the heaven I hoped for,
not what I wanted at all.
Why are corporate heads
not rolling
in sludge
spilled from their own factories?
Or millionaires reaching for peaches
that hang just out of touch
as their hunger gnaws
like a beaver
at every nerve
and desire increases ceaselessly
and always with compound interest?

I imagined a rocky summit
with a parade of weary CEO's
marching up a slippery mountainside
lugging heavy barrels to nowhere.
But now I see where the boulder of Sisyphus
has collided with an Exxon tanker
and the birds of prey
are coated in thick black crude
unable to reach the men playing with fire,
and we're all distracted
by gunfire, crack wars,
and lovers dying
to notice how richly patterned
the silver is at banquets
where tycoons and tyrants
share small talk on distant perches,
warning the rest of us
not to fly
too close
to the sun.

To My Rapist

When you rub my breasts
and grab between my thighs
I clamp my legs imagining them scissors.

When your fingers run
through my hair and pull tight
I want to bite off each digit.

When you wrap my hand
around your thickened rod of flesh
I wish I had a knife to flay your skin.

When you yank my head to your groin
and plunge a silencer
into my screams

I imagine myself a kitchen sink,
my heartbeat motoring
the disposal of your dick.

When you drive yourself full force
between my legs
I wish I had a shotgun barrel

to shove up your tightened ass
another to shove down your throat
your own climax on the trigger

so bullets meet in the middle
mixing blood and semen
near your heartlessness.

When you thrust
and thrust and thrust
who can count?

When it is over for you
my breasts turn to scabs.
I drown in anything liquid.

Into the door you opened
bottles, daggers, sticks—
anything long and hard threatens entrance.

When I think of you now
I want you in a hell
where at every moment

every cell in
your body is
pried open

by loving hands
that burn with flames
of violation.

Domestic Bliss

Our cupboard echoes with laughter
from dinner parties
to which we were never invited

the bookshelves are lined with
unfriendly litanies, hostile histories,
and an alien atlas that maps no place for us

the ashes of our grandmothers' hopes
lightly dust the dresser top
and a mountain of soiled laundry

piles high in the corner of the room
until the only home I know
is your smile

Ocean Air

—For all who have ever had to invent
ways of making their love valid, official
or visible to the world

Here silent dunes witness my farewell
to what we let lawyers write you as:
son and, therefore, heir
to what we built together.

Here I take law in hand
and set to flame
the last reminder of our fear
that my family would erase you and take all.

I burn the only evidence
that I am father,
that you
are my son.

Let these ashes dissolve
in ocean waves
while the sand lays claim to stories
traced by our embraces on the shore.

Here no mourners stare
at the silk green fish tie
I wore for your funeral.
The one you gave when I turned forty.

Here no caskets close
on the lipless smile—
explosion of teeth bursting out
from beneath rough mustache and beard.

Memory stands open to the moment
I discovered your lips with mine
and explored each pearl of you
with my tongue.

Here no priest tells me
how to remember you
as I set in bronze the memory of
your long calves and thighs laced with mine.

Here only flowers grow wild
beside the hidden stretch of sand
where you first leaned hard against me
while smoothing lotion on my back.

You reached past my shoulder
down my chest to feel
if I was hard too,
and I was.

We found joyful release together
on the beach under the midday sun.
The sounds and spray of ocean
indistinguishable from our own.

Now as sun sets a crimson horizon to bed
I see the same red glow that rose in your cheek
every time the spotted puppy you named "Holstein"
stood erect to hump a visitor's leg.

Here my breathing is marked
by the heavy pant of an aging dalmatian
who now only raises an eye
when visitors call.

I was certain
I would be first to go,

so I bought the dog for you,
to keep you from ever being alone.

But I had already passed on too much.

Now I watch the last flicker
shake itself out in the ocean air.
A puff of smoke and ash
trailing off to sea.

Here and now returns us
to what we have been all along:
man and man sharing a love
more durable than blood.

The Journey

If the shortest path
is a straight line,
I will be late.

The Divine Is Here

When I search the star-filled heavens
for knowledge of God,
the moon offers
only the hollow outline of my own body
stretched black across a glowing field.
I see that light and shadow are one.

When I dream myself to the base
of a canyon,
bands of soil paint
the river's age up walls of sandstone
as water washes earth to new shape.
I know that death and birth are one.

When the sunlight dances itself alive
on the river,
beside me is a lizard
who sleeps in the blazing heat
only because it feels right to touch the sun.
I feel that dream and spirit are one.

When the river winds out of sight
in time's tendency to bend
that which is straight,
gravity's natural pull
keeps the quickest currents at the outer edge.
I taste why I am where I am.

When I breathe
to the quiet breeze
it breathes back to me
as she does
when we hold each other close.
I believe in the power of touch.

I search, I dream, the sunlight dances,
and the divine is here
in the midnight sky
at the water's edge,
in a shared breath,
and in her loving eyes.

The Muse

woman announcing her perfect self
juggling the stars and lifting the sky
she waves the clouds like a flag across the galaxies
holding the ocean in cupped hands
to drink in life and love in one womanly swallow
she takes root in the earth
and her womb fills with rainbows
she embodies birth and spirit and breath
anointing her brothers with honey and fire
showering her sisters with the spray of sunshine
sprinkling desert sand upon her children
she gathers glaciers volcanos and waterfalls to her breast
and builds an eternity with each new syllable
calling forth all her mothers and fathers
robed in the simple radiance of being
she reaches for nothing that is not already part of her
as her harmonies house the entire cosmos

Censorship's Enemy

"The straightjacket on my tongue
frees me to explain how silence kills,"
she said, speaking to save her own life.

Final Draft

warm breath of summerkissed wind
caressable contours of an Olympian's pose
gentle strength of enveloping hold
passionate glow on a love-locked brow
rivery flow of quicksilver sweetness
spiralling intensity of smoothsilken touch
shared explosion of inner selves
absolute completion of two souls merging
windborn visions of flames on ice converging
fantasy flies through moonbeam skies
astrology anatomy telepathy anarchy
governing regions outside inside above and under
tightening frightening screaming thunder
streaming lightning dreaming wonder
centigrade turns Fahrenheit
temperature rises
I write
my editor quickly revises
I accept almost all
he ever advises
the rhyme
the rhythm
I rewrite to please him
my poem complete
I patiently wait
still unpublished
"unfinished" he says
until I get the final word straight
but the pronoun resists the slightest revising
undiminished unending and uncompromising
one pronoun persists in action and word
loud proud and insistent on being heard
reliant and forceful continually growing
defiant resourceful openly showing

now always forever before and after
in sickness and health
in tears and laughter
my affection
I trust
is no small whim
my love
my lust
my poem
is for
her

Knowing Who I Am

To nuzzle between warm breasts
To tease a nipple with my tongue
To witness a childbirth
To bathe in a sea of cum

is to sing the sacred
is to tend a garden
is to set sail with menstrual tides
is to celebrate the woman I am

All Tenderness

Each moment of loving
rides as a droplet
down the shores of my body
drifting across the surface of time
until all tenderness shared
suspends itself in the wet of my memory
                              No act of love can be lost
Each touch liquifies
losing itself in an ocean
of loss and gain
where time's passages
twist memory
into new shapes
like
        blackfish submerging
            leviathan rising
                jellyfish prickling
                    dolphins colliding
                        anglers enticing
                            anemone tickling
                                starfish and terrapin
                                momentarily hiding
                                by cautiously clinging
                                to coral and sand
        but memories
(no more lasting than the moments themselves)
        never find permanent hiding or rest
        at the bottom
            of a bottomless
                borderless sea

The tides of a soul shift
but the waters grow richer and wider
with each moment laughed or cried

225

Embraces settle
stir
and settle again

only until
the next kiss of wind
sweeps the sea—
storms spin memories to surface
frothy curls build to arched waves
breakers crash back into themselves

but the soft overhead pull of the moon
the patterned flow of ancient currents
and the infinite mysteries of one's own depth
keep all love alive
and all life loved

Legacies

—In appreciation of the work of honest historians like Lillian Faderman

The branches of our tribal tree
burned pink flames as kindling
beneath the women of Salem,
women guilty of living without men
committing the spinster crime
of independence.

We are heir to the fear
that hung a queer shadow
over the shuttered house in Amherst
where a brave woman wrote of another:

> *Her heart is fit for home—*
> *I—a Sparrow—build there*
> *Sweet of twigs and twine*
> *My perennial nest.*

critics insisting
"The persona is a male sparrow."

By my own birthright,
I will dwell in more than possibility
and shape my nests in ways
the songbirds of the Berkshires
reserved only for poetry.
To hell with the critics!

> *"Susie, will you indeed come*
> *home next Saturday,*
> *and be my own again,*
> *and kiss me as you used to?"*

But Emily, you sent those words in secret
to the woman who later married
your brother
and your estate kept the letters
in some distant cupboard after your death.
The textbooks tell
how you turned recluse
when abandoned by the man you loved.
Another mad woman in the closet.

From the spark of my own strength
I try to speak in flames
that resurrect witches.

The teenage daughter of a friend
sees me at a gay pride rally
"What are you doing here?" she asks.
I am pinkly dressed to the hightops.

Overjoyed to find a role model her parents know,
she tells of isolation at home
and ridicule at school.
"How do you handle name-calling?"
she wants to know.

Shall I tell her how I trembled
when a drunk in a holiday town
saw me laughing?
An intimate laugh perhaps
no touching, just a laugh
with my girlfriend.
He thrust his face in mine
screaming on Main Street,
right in front of a cop:

> *"You need a real man!*
> *You need a fuck!*

I was a fuckin' fighter pilot in 'Nam!
I'll show you a real man!
Fuck you!"

The policeman walked the other way.

The drunken voice echoes
in the ashes of my forefathers:
forty-thousand gay men
rounded up by the Gestapo
accused and convicted of loving
branded with pink triangles
yoked by hard labor
and finally corralled.

That young woman's refrain:
"How do you handle name-calling?"

What is there to pass on
to the children of the clan
who try suicide at triple the rate of others?

Let no one inherit the closet.

My kinship is not about cheekbones,
genetics, or family picnics.
Ours is an alliance
rooted in defiance
strengthened by politics
sustained in spite of opposition
and renewed by love.

The Persistence of Pink

Pink was ballet shoes
doll clothes
hair ribbons
and flowers.

Barrettes and balloons
pencil erasers and yarn,
the bow on my first training bra
was pink.

Pink had no vote in Senate.
It was never in the news.
Appearing as an afterthought,
pink was a suffix tacked on.

Pink was the princess
who spoke only to cry "help"
so the prince in shining armor—
not pink—could save her.

Pink lacked sincerity—
Birthday cards
from aunts and uncles
never seen.

Boys wouldn't touch it.
Sports teams never wore it.
Nothing fast was pink,
Nothing strong or with power.

Pink didn't get dirty
Pink never got loud
or rough or rowdy.
It couldn't run or kick or throw.

Pink alerted the non-pink
to inferiority. A warning label:
Beware the fragile nature
of the weak pink soul.

So I pitied pink.
Avoided its soft fabrics
and cheap plastic goods.
Who ever saw pink leather or steel?

Pink had nothing to offer me
but the constant reminder
of who cooked, who cleaned,
who knitted, who cheered.

So I abandoned pink
to live as greyly as I could.
But even when I closed my eyes
pink would not let go.

Pink announced itself in sunsets.
Pink called to me by name.
Pink took a zillion shapes and shades,
so no two looked the same.

Loud pinks
dark light neon
soft and bright pinks
hot pink pastel lavender and rose pink.

Pink marched beside me,
pink anger, pink pride.
Pink hornpiped in the streets
as pink lightning tore the sky.

I loved pink's flash and daring.
Pink took risks, broke every rule.

Pink could be soft and round and cuddly
or angular, brash, blinding.

I celebrated all the ways of pink
that danced in people's lives
and once I loved the pink around me
I embraced the pink inside.

I Am Not Outrageous

I am not outrageous
enough
for my mother to ask why my sheets
are satin and my underwear crotchless
for my sister to untie the tampons
that dangle above my dashboard
like a pair of fuzzy dice
for my father to throw out
the diaphragm rotting on my window sill
for my brother to steal
the pen from between
my teeth

My future reclines
schizophrenic on the couch—
content, conversant,
but unconscious
to the multiple tongues
that lash out
lick in
lay down
leap tall buildings in a single bound
and laugh aloud
with every breath
that escapes these lips

Too many lovers, landlords
and lobotomies
have carved through me
like shark fins slicing the sea

Scars disappear
as quickly as they come

and I tell my doctor
his fly is unzipped
when it isn't

I am not outrageous
enough
to shake the stars
salt the cities
swallow the flames
flatten the earth
or make a difference
for anyone
except myself
and until I inspire anarchy
I am not outrageous
enough

Printed September 1992 in Santa Barbara & Ann
Arbor for the Black Sparrow Press by Mackintosh
Typography & Edwards Brothers Inc. Text set in
Bodoni by Words Worth. Design by Barbara Martin.
This edition is published in paper wrappers;
there are 200 hardcover trade copies;
125 hardcover copies have been numbered & signed
by the author; & 26 copies handbound in boards
by Earle Gray are lettered & signed by the author.

Photo: Tim Morse

NANCY BOUTILIER spent her childhood in Northborough, Massachusetts wearing black high-top sneakers before it was fashionable. She told her fifth-grade teacher she was going to play for the Harlem Globetrotters, and when she realized she wasn't tall enough for the NBA, Nancy set her sights on being a poet. She completed Basic Training at Fort Knox, Kentucky, and she now tries hard not to use any of the skills she learned there. A sharpshooter with an M-16 rifle, Nancy still tends to dangle modifiers. She has never learned to knit, but she is good with paint and clever political slogans challenging militarism. She attended Harvard/Radcliffe College and the Bread Loaf School of English. Currently a high school English teacher, Nancy officiates basketball games and writes during half-time. She contributes regularly to the *Bay Area Reporter*, and her work has also appeared in *Sphere, OUT/LOOK, Deneuve,* and *Girljock.* Nancy hopes she is finally tall enough.